This poetry carries a hand-full of soft stones that sink and surface, shiver between decomposition and preservation as she dries herself to recall movement through surfaces beneath and above them. This is a sustained interrogation of the construction of a self that is intricate; intimate as much as broad ranged; larger than the pool the poet enters; and up against melancholy as a prospectus on beauty or the unattainable. The poem compels attention to itself as it expands, alliterates, rhymes, moves off at tangent and is wonderfully obsessive. Pool is polis and micro-thought, dense and reconciled. It demands frailty and errors of perception that become portentous and then elusive in moth flickers, expansive and pulled into itself, frightened and pervasive. The book celebrates a powerful engagement.
*Allen Fisher*

**By the same author**

*ikszedik stáció* (Universitas, Budapest, 2000)

*Medalion* (Universitas, Budapest, 2002)

*Budapest to Babel* (Egg Box Publishing, 2008)

*Poetry, The Geometry of The Living Substance – Four Essays on Ágnes Nemes Nagy* (Cambridge Scholars, 2011)

*Rememberer* (Egg Box Publishing, 2012)

*Carillonneur* (Shearsman Books, 2014)

*Palimpszeszt* (Magyar Napló, Budapest, 2015)

*Poems from the Swimming Pool* (Constitutional Information, Sheffield, 2015)

*Pool Epitaphs and Other Love Letters* (Boiler House Press, 2017)

Ágnes Lehóczky

**Swimming Pool**

Shearsman Books

First published in the United Kingdom in 2017
by Shearsman Books
50 Westons Hill Drive
Emersons Green
BRISTOL
BS16 7DF

Shearsman Books Ltd Registered Office
30-31 St. James Place, Mangotsfield, Bristol BS16 9JB
*(this address not for correspondence)*

www.shearsman.com
ISBN 978-1-84861-542-7

[Postcard 1], 'It's time, A...' (p.15) copyright © Adam Piette, 2017.

[Postcard 2], 'Time How Short' (p.51)
copyright © Denise Riley, 2017.

[Postcard 3], 'The second of September, a card from Switzerland'
(p.85) copyright © Terry O'Connor, 2017.

Remainder of the book copyright © Ágnes Lehóczky, 2017.

The right of Ágnes Lehóczky to be identified as the author of this
work has been asserted by her in accordance with the Copyrights,
Designs and Patents Act of 1988.
All rights reserved.

Cover photo:
*Untitled #7, 2002* (from *The Pool* series) – Karine Laval

Design and typesetting
Miklós Ferencz
Text and titles are set in Freight Text Pro
Cover title is set in Freight Micro Pro

Photo by Noé

# Contents

| | |
|---|---|
| **Book One: On the Swimming Pool** | 13 |
| [Postcard 1] *For A., a sauterelle* | 15 |
| Word One | 17 |
| Hypnos and Hajnóczy | 18 |
| On the Swimming Pool | 21 |
| Melancholy Swimmer | 28 |
| Enunciation | 32 |
|    The Rhetorical Swimmer | 32 |
|    The Museologist Swimmer | 33 |
|    The Polyglot Swimmer | 36 |
| Rockenbauer, the Diver | 39 |
| The *Mother* | 42 |
| | |
| **Book Two: Pool Epitaphs and Other Love Letters** | 49 |
| [Postcard 2] *Time How Short* | 51 |
| [† Prologos: [Apostil 1 / Illuminations 1]; I:1] 'And so when we enter the swimming pool' | 53 |
| [Pool Epitaph i; letter I:13] '…And so on a hot August day' | 54 |
| [PE ii; letter II:13] '…Dear silent swimmer *sans* silhouette' | 56 |
| [PE iii; letter III:13] '…And the now was always already pool' | 58 |
| [PE iv; letter IV:13] '…Apo phainesthai ta phainomena' | 59 |
| [PE v; letter V:13] 'For the poem is grotesque' | 61 |
| [PE vi; letter VI:13] '…Viva carcass' | 62 |
| [PE vii; letter VII:13] '…A month later, on a heartfelt, heartless day' | 64 |
| [PE viii; letter VIII:13] '…Look, I think dead artists are' | 65 |
| [PE ix; letter IX:13] '…Dear floating flâneur' | 67 |
| [PE x; letter X:13] '…Dear non-swimmer' | 70 |
| [PE xi; letter XI:13] '… Apo phainesthai ta phainomena' | 72 |
| [PE xii; letter XII:13] '… Last Sunday you sent me' | 74 |
| [PE xiii; letter XIII:13] 'Viva la pool' | 76 |
| [ ‡ Postscript, Miscellanea; I:1] 'Torch bearer, faithful concierge' | 77 |

| | |
|---|---|
| **Book Three: Fall of Pool** | **83** |
| [Postcard 3] *The second of September, a card from Switzerland* | **85** |
| Part One: Letters from Lacrima | **87** |
| [The Swimmers' Discourse] | **89** |
| [Pool letter 1.1 typed, Misc. i] | **90** |
| [On Catastrophe] | **91** |
| [Pool letter 1.2 typed, Misc. ii] | **94** |
| [Pool letter 1.3 typed, Misc. iii] | **95** |
| [On Fear] | **96** |
| [Pool letter 1.4 typed, Misc. iv] | **102** |
| [Pool letter 1.5 typed, Misc. v] | **103** |
| [Chronicles of Shame] | **104** |
| [Pool letter 1.6 typed, Misc. vi] | **112** |
| [On the Poet's House] | **113** |
| [Pool letter 1.7 typed, Misc. vii] | **117** |
| Part Two: On the Art of Tautologising | **119** |
| [Pool letter 1.8 typed, Misc. viii] | **120** |
| [Letter from Terry] | **121** |
| [On Another Death of the Moth] | **123** |
| [Pool letter 1.9 typed, Misc. ix] | **125** |
| [On the Glass Poem] | **126** |
| [On the Sepia Swimmer] | **131** |
| [On Matt's Spirit Duplicator] | **135** |
| [Pool letter 1.10 typed, Misc. x] | **137** |
| **Acknowledgements** | **139** |

*For Adam Piette, the anonymous author, the hydrophilic friend*

*Swimming Pool*

*Discourse on Correlations in Water*

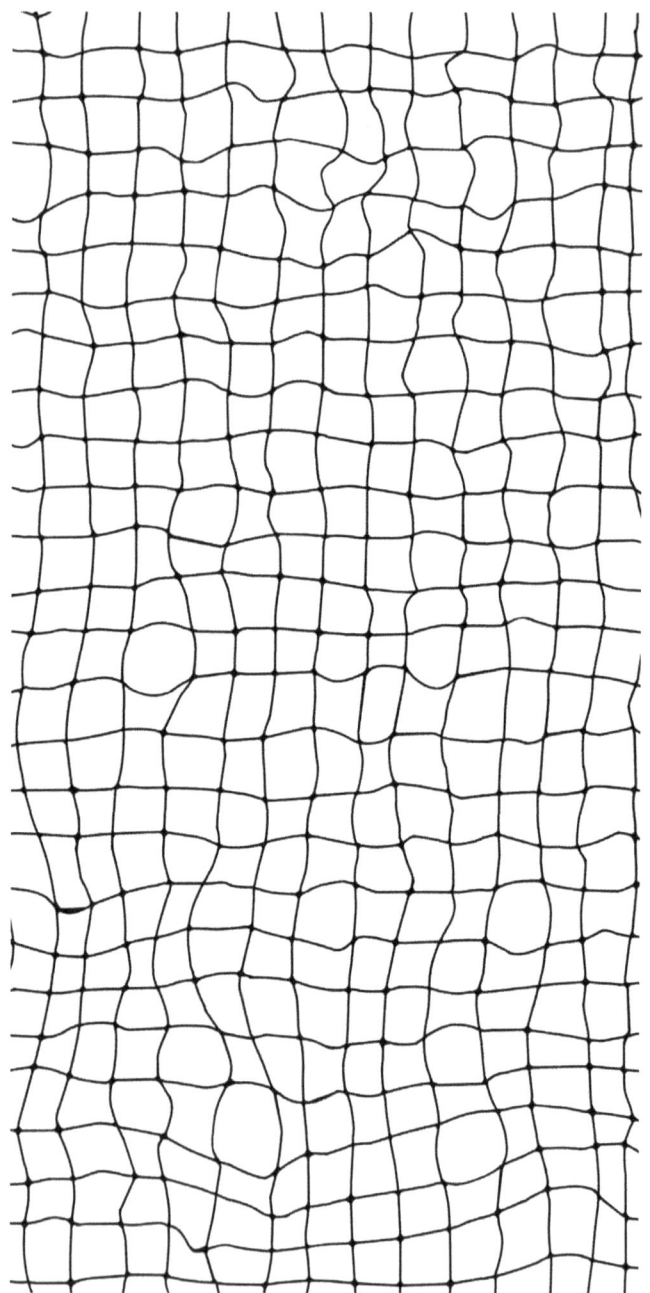

*Book One*

**On the Swimming Pool**

[Postcard 1]

**It's** time, A., you should really check the time –
**Sweet** time! & in the sparkling depths of the pool,
**Friend**, enjoy liquefactions of desire;
**To** swim & immerse the embodied mind.
**Swim** your heart & soul out, all those lengths,
**In** such a joyful blue transparency!
**Pool** o pool, from the Danube to the Don,
**As** names writ in water, flow like language
**Night**! Day! through all the blue temporalities
**Falls** the leaping figure on A\*\*\*\*'s day ...

Adam Piette, 'For A., a sauterelle'

**Word One**

The word (*word One* in this language) begins with Ἄλφα in the other's alphabet. Its prior symbol like a letter A tilted on its side, suspended in air and time, is now morphed into swimming pool, a priori. Indigo rorschach on an electronic postcard designed and sent by Adam on the occasion of my return to England. Those days I talked much about swimming as search for correlations between two parabola poles. And it's because the swimming pool is yet another aporia. Thinking de profundis. Thinking of punctuation. Ending the sentence by drowning. Àpropos of melancholia. Or even more superfluous. Narcissistic. A universal weakness. The desire to navigate the body home through language. Pathology of the poem through pathos is what it is. The document, a liquefied polis, when I first received it, later read as an exported artwork from *procreate*. And millennia later I stuck the sheet on the white wall of my office in Sheffield. I also laminated this landscape. So that it could preserve its purpose once and for all without morphing into somewhere else (such as Glossop Road Baths just off West Street or The Rawson Spring in Hillsborough, these liminalities with fluid functions inhabited by one's own fluid selves). This I shall soon send to you in another's attachments. The glossy paper *now* portrays a blue canvas textured like waves and currents shaped like miniature curly tongues. Apo phainesthai ta phainomena. You could almost recognise the chequered tiles flickering at the bottom of this pool. The attachment *then* was entitled *Escaping Time*. This, perhaps, will always already be a one-way correspondence with the anonymous author, the hydrophilic friend. One in which one is at the receiving end.

**Hypnos and Hajnóczy**

Hypnos, the hydrophilic scribe writes in one summer email with a postcard attached on which Hypnos is lying divinely on his side with his half-brother, addressed to me along with many other addressees whose name I could not recognise at the time, turned up at the pool the other day. I have come to understand a posteriori, the message reads on, that there are simple correlations between the pool milieu and the mood of the elegiac. Between exercising the body and the movement of desire, one's perpetual drive to lead organic life back to its inanimate state; to magna mater: o water, the swimmer writes. O writing. Perhaps swimming, my anonymous reader, is the ultimate attraction towards the phlegmatic, to possibilities of thinking without punctuation, *sans* full stops. Imagine the pool, like one's inner washing machine, a hollow drum running in logocentric circles laundryless, weightless, in cyclical aquatic murmurs. In city thinking is concrete. Have you too felt that resilience in you towards anything too tangible, too definitive, and too well-defined? O the fluid statics of the swimming body, the thought, the clinamen together at rest and in motion. The poem's desire to refuse to understand anything premeditated at all. Look. Sebald's peripatetic walk occurs all along the East Anglian seashore picking up remnants of the memory of the melancholic no-one. This uncanny unnameable follows us to most places, from isles to isles, from pool to pool. From script to script. The attraction to drowning in the polis for the first time. The imprint of this event, always already sui generis, is inerasable. We don't know what it is but we know that it's waiting. And when we don't know is when we wear the knowing face, head bowed down, raking through the clutter of East Anglian (apocalyptic) shorelines. But, anonymous friend, in our discourse with the swimmer, the lover, one should aspire to more from these melancholic meanderings during which you had long lost whom you had sought. Recycle the wealth of the waste word. The saminess of the soul structure. The simulacrum of the cosmos. O, water ball, the globe. The hopelessness in which we rejoice, viva cul-de-sac; *sans* chance to find the beginning or the end always already unending, looking back at seashores always already in advance or strolling on large pebbles, who knows why, but always already backwards. False-etymology might help to open the gulf of such orphic syllogisms. Take the example of Hypnos and Hajnóczy and their binary opposition, Hypnos and his (for now) twin brother, the post-modern author, the alcoholic anonymous. *Death Rode Out of Persia* is largely set in an outdoor swimming pool in Budapest in the 1970s written from the perspective of the unreliable narrator, a former swimmer, who spends most of his time in the pool, resting carefree on his elbow drinking cans of lager and numerous brandy shots. Hajnóczy (in whose tragic case smooth-sighing Apollo is conquered by the wine drinking goat-like centaur), whose life ended due to liver failure at the age of thirty eight, is crucial for us in this line of thinking. Hypnos, who never sees the sun, lives his or her life in the cave of swimmers unminding original thought. This cultural amnesia, coralised underwater, is the paradox of modernity, the philosopher says. Hajnóczy's protagonist like a centaur, half-merged in the underworld, exercising a difficult breathing exercise, some tragicomic version of katabasis, longs for magna mater, for the cosmic womb, the absolute hydrostatic equilibrium, for the ultimate paradox. When he begins his novel, he says he needs an awfully large white paper to fill with language. To be able to ever terminate the book. To both be motion on the page, and idle. He thinks by spending time in the pool he will escape the opening sentence, his own addiction, his drive against language too phlegmatic to ever stop. Pool for the unnamed protagonist is bohemia and beer, dreamy dates, sepia changing cabins and sleepy cityscape. Pool is warm earth and another anonymous self. Or perhaps pool is mask. A surgical mask, a swimming mask. Pool a death mask. A theatre mask worn by one's inner protagonist in a larger story lying stylishly on his side on hot ink-blue tiles while the story itself around him unfolds. Pool the masquerade. A summer nap. Human fluid, heated temperament. The effigy of bronze bodies. A boundless afternoon banter on water temperature, the availability of

sunbeds and brilliant weather. Another brilliant banquet. But there is more to it. He also thinks pool is enlightenment, the possibility of all artless combinations of nonsensical thoughts and correlations; pool the absolute trope. Pool: trope's *aw*ful absence. There is no real separation between the swimming body and equilibrium. O silent friend *sans* soul, these thoughts are only one length apart; dependent on the fitness of the lungs. We must let the poem to and fro and to and fro in a hydraulic freedom for a lifetime, and when necessary allow it to struggle breathlessly like Woolf's moth on the glass, the no chance moth, the helpless moth, an anonymous dead moth which then gains a second life in an essay posthumously published in 1942. We, naturally, talk of a posthumous moth after all, struggling for its life on the window, always already in advance. Although one can't help feeling that the long-winded scrutiny of the moth is unnecessarily relentless and that the unknown narrator could have saved the lepidopteran with a simple movement. Did she in the end become fascinated by watching the furry thing dying for long hours? And besides, if she had bothered to save the moth's life with a simple fluid movement, that heart soaring article could have never been written after all? O the pathos. The bath(os). The gymnos. Body parameters.
The entrance into the body's end through a swimming pool length. Here, if you will, when we trespass our own borders (say *by sentence*) we enter the maze of the Great Eastern Hotel near Liverpool Street station. We enter and take a seat next to a table opposite the louvered windows. We sit and watch the author sitting and watching. He is sipping his drink away slowly, slowly staring at us through his metachromatic mind. And the room begins to swim away with you and the anonymous author in its own artificial light.

## On the Swimming Pool

...but we must, the anonymous author continues,
pause at this absolute city – the Pool. The total polis
whose job is to await you, silent correspondent; pool
the every polis that awaits the other too. Pool a
nocturnal polis. Pool patient. Pool patient polis. Pool
the democratic. Pool Parthenon. Pool an unmarried
woman's apartment. Pool marginal. Pool eccentric.
Pool *my* temple. Pool her sovereign cell. Pull the full.
Pool to the full. Complete. Pool pars pro toto. Pool the
western *cella* of a much larger pool. The much larger
pool the unconscious of the city. Pool that never
drains. Pool undrains, Eliot says, brown edged where
the lotos rose. Pool agora. Pool assembles. Pool where
one *speaks* in thoughts. Pool the once crowded central
market Socrates failed to take me to in winter. The one
that now floats in regret and aggravation. Regret and
silence. Pool is not for agoraphobics. Pool is also
where Socrates used to lean outside, waiting for me to
come out at last. But that was a long time ago. Pool is
now. So pool Botanical Gardens Clarkehouse Road
S10 2LN in the organic city. Pool another garden in
this Botanical Garden or that Botanical Garden. Pool
is Barker's Pool with the 90 foot tall war memorial
erected at its focus. Pool as parthenon the highest
point in town, reservoir, lemon balm, drinking water
and water supply to cleanse the city's streets,
youngsters, dogs and pigs, houses, windows, ginnels
and cul-de-sacs four times a year. If pool cleanses the
polis pool will cleanse you of your own glossic guilt.
Pool where language speaks instead of you. De
profundis. It's a laminated postcard from the pool.
Pool is public shower rooms where you can stand for
hours waiting to be cleansed. Deafened by the
dictation of writing in water. O all the books published
in the pool. Pool is Library, books you'll never write
or regret ever having written. Pool is Theatre. Pool is

re-entering the world feeling filthy all over again. Pool is Citadel, water containing oxygen. Pool is Heidegger's *horizon*. Pool is coins. Pool is coins in a pool. Pool is pocket money. Pool is (my) Capital. Pool is cathedral. But not the one in Sheffield. Pool explored in *Swimming Studies* by Leanne Shapton (an imprint of Penguin). Pool is a penguin. Pool is a universal whale. Pool is the dome of Cologne surviving all apocalypses both in the future and the past. Pool is cosmopolis, astropolis, ecumenopolis, megapolis. Pool is necropolis and pool is heliopolis too. Heliopolis for the hydrophilic. I am a hydrophilic. Pool in Sheffield is steelopolis. The term Metalopolis has been used already for another polis. Pool Holy City. Pool my hieropolis. Pool citta eterna from Greek *rhèo* or Latin *ruo* both meaning 'flow'. Pool everything and everywhere. It is this hieropolis where Adam will chant 'Viva Pool'. Pool is not what you think it is. Pool is certainly not what *I* thinks it is. Pool is what you are thinking. Pool is what I am thinking too. Pool populus. Pool the identity-free crowd. Pool a crowd with free identity. Pool is plans to process. From hydrophilia (via acrophobia) to pool is concrete-phobia. Pool a large tap. Pool alcoholics anonymous. Pool essentially water but pool with four walls. Pool boggy land. Pool the eerie abstract landscape. Pool Cardigan Bay from which a prehistoric forest emerges one day, where Geraldine&Alan once will have stood in long winter coats staring at skeletal oak, pine, alder and birch tree trunks not noticing the watchful photographer taking a photo of them from afar that appears in the Guardian in February without their consent or knowledge. Pool, the enclosed garden Louise dips into in her essay on 'Cultural Centring of Catalan Swimming Pools', reads almost like a pool poem. Pool is airport. Pool the seaport. Pool a gymnasium with a crowd of gymnos. Pool is Jean-Jacques Rousseau. Pool the river where the nameless ornithologist loses her phone and dives after it managing to rescue the sim-card. Somewhere in Derbyshire in September. Pool Budapest. Pool nakedness. O the dressing and undressing. All the costumes and the costumelessness. Pool the other skin. Pool imitation. The competitive anonymous other. Pool and its own chain of command. Micro-societal. Pool a Neolithic pictograph. Pool cinema. Pool citizenship. Pool the Pool of Tears. Pool the Darwinian at times. Pool, you are Empson. Pool you are full of Dodos and Mice and Monkeys. Pool is either a competition or a splash session (with Sigmund Freud) in a competition slash leisure pool. Pool is wunderkammer, the precursor of museums full of stuffed fish and corals. Pool objects in order: plastic kayaks, canoes, ropes, and red-and white life-belts all waiting here to let go of their contours and become themselves. Pool paraphernalia. Pool hierarchy and administration. Pool technology. Pool both death and life drive. Pool the aquatic dream machine. Pool both innocent and hostile neon light. Pool the first polis. Pool the last polis. Pool the sky turned upside down. Pool is eternal since pool is already dead. Pool is Pericles' visionary city. Pool unrealistic, absurd, therefore exists. As opposed to divine. Pool the phenomenology of fluid; the physiology of time liquefied in a green bottle neck. There is time for being in the water is body for being in the world. Pool the choice of goggles through which you take a look at this world. In pool the speed mirrored goggles with anti-fog panoramic lenses give you enhanced peripheral vision. This also allows you to see the world while the world cannot see you. But sometimes in pool even the anti-fog lenses can get steamed-up from the inside. And you can bleed internally, anonymously, even to death - without a name. Pool is where one posits him or herself as a vertebrate or an amphibian. Pool ars poetica. Pool the immersion in the world. So pool the body. Pool the many bodies. Pool embodiment. Pool knowledge of one's alternate body weight and body length. Recognition of pressure on skin. Pool the weightless psyche of a boy God

Socrates asked me to photograph in Athens. Or the sleeping woman at Ambelokipi, stood in the middle of Mavili Square; around her oranges and urban pigeons scattered.

Pool, Eliot says, is down the passage which we did not take. Through the first gate into our first world, along the empty alley, filled with water out of sunlight. And they were behind us, reflected in the pool. Then a cloud passed, and the pool was empty. Pool tabula rasa. Pool utopia. Pool heterotopia. Pool the ahistorical. The asexual. Pool dissymmetry. Pool asymmetry. Ahistory. Pool the personal history turned upside down. Pool the genderless for pool is clothelessness. But pool Speedo or Arena. Pool athletic sportswear. If pool is populus & industry then pool enactment. Its role is to house the Olympic team sponsored by Arena. But the anonymous *I* in pool prefers Speedo and questions pool's absolute goodness from time to time wondering whether pool were simulacrum. To make any statement about a pool won't ever be possible. Pool always already all possibilities. Improbabilities. Pool tautology. Pool heteroglossia. Pool glossolalia. Pool the female shower room crowded with elderly Yorkshire women all talking at once. The best is that you can still speak when your mouth is full of pool. Viva the pool, viva

Pool. Pool is where you, the swimmer, can become a polyglot. Pool is where you speak no language(s) and it is also where you speak them all. Pool echolalia. Pool the deaf world. Pool is someone lying at the bottom of the pool. Pool is you lying dead at the bottom of the pool. Pool is Paul Klee's angel staring back at you from the bottom of the pool. Distancing. Distancing. Slowly. Slowly. Away from the pool. Pool present. Pool past. Pool is *Death Rode Out of Persia*, written by the dead author, the anonym alcoholic who prefers water to writing. He finds it easier, somewhat lighter. Pool dead language. Pool the second language. Pool unlike language at all. All syntactic combinations possible in water. Nothing, too, is possible in pool. If all this fails at least pool is freedom of thought in pool. Pool all personal, pool all political, pool collective, pool civic. Pool motions, pool idles, too. The other day a hydrophilic friend chose pool instead of heated conversation about Scottish referendum. I read this on the pool's online public forum. Pool choice. But pool idea. Pool the ideal. Pool the anti-Platonic. Pool democracy. Pool anti-perspiration. You still can sweat in pool; it just goes unnoticed. Pool rarely bloodbath. Pool the bloodbath in the 1956 Melbourne Olympics Water Polo semi-final. Pool the Suez Canal British troops are wading through during the water polo match in Melbourne. Pool atemporality. For pool an erased word. Pool the unnameable. Pool is unnameables although you can pronounce it with one breath. In the other's language it's pronounced with two. Pool is irritating alteration times. Pool ordered timetables, too. Pool punctuation. Pool is not where you learn to swim. Pool is where you swim. Pool is where you think. Pool is the hut in the Black Forest with Heidegger hiding while a storm rages outside. Pool is business at times. Pool water polis. Pool is what I look for. Pool calendar. Pool the valediction of weeping according to John Donne. Pool is the British Isles Roger Deakin set out in 1996 to swim through. Pool fluid flânerie. Pool topography, calligraphy, cartography. Pool the river Danube, passing through four capital cities, discharging itself into the Black Sea, the one which Anonymous Author always wants to bathe in. I never told my hydrophilic friend that grandfather used to stand by the bank of this river watching the non-swimmers of the continent floating downwards towards the sea. The Danube which Madeleine thought is so shallow that boats navigate it with wheels touching the bottom. Pool black pool. The river into which Paul ran naked, hungover one August evening, overheated, sunstruck. Study of water and pool concrete. O the aquatic flâneur and his private view of an island race and a people with a deep affinity for water. From the sea, from rock pools, from rivers and streams, tarns, lakes, lochs, ponds, lidos, swimming pools and spas, from fens, dykes, moats, aqueducts, waterfalls, flooded quarries, even canals. Pool is where Deakin gets detained by water bailiffs in Winchester, intercepted in the Fowey estuary by coastguards, mistaken for a suicide on Camber sands, confronting the Corryvreckan whirlpool in the Hebrides. Pool a personal blind map. Pool cycle. Pool the spasmodic beeping of the clock on the arena's wall. Pool the life cycle of an eighty-two year old swimming pool in Cambridge captured in a documentary through the work of artist across four seasons. Pool that just *is*. Pool is where you are. Pool is where I'd always want to be. Pool is where I always am. Sometimes pool just isn't. Pool John Cheever the swimmer. Egerszegi, or Darnyi. Pool cultural and natural history. Pool is public conversations. Pool is current news. Pool many pools at the same time. Pool, on the other hand, is your local swimming pool. My hydrophilic friend's is Ponds Forge or Goodwin in Sheffield, and Komjádi in Budapest. Which one do you go to? Pool anthropology. Pool the eureka moment of all body parts including brain and lungs. Pool elementary skill. Pool awaits you, silent correspondent. Pool is a polis that awaits your arrival late into the night. Pool is a nocturnal polis. Pool patient. Pool cosmos. Pool cosmology. Pool planetary. Pool part but wholly part of you. For pool is never jealous. Pool is never boastful or conceited. Pool sometimes is full of plastic boats. Pool at night is full of other planets. Pool is tough when pool is waterpolo. Although pool is tough pool always plays fairplay. Pool never plays a foul play. For pool is never rude or selfish. Pool is mainly summer. For pool is not resentful. Pool delights in truth and light. Pool is always ready to excuse, to trust, to hope, and to endure whatever comes. Pool the mopped up tiled corridor and changing room. Pool the cleaning lady early winter morning who endures whatever comes. Pool is winter. Pool is winterization. Pool migration. Pool builds new polis in which there will always be new pools. Pool the creative. Pool the prehistoric. Pool post-historic. Pool autumn, spring. Pool is never histrionic. Pool pastoral. Pool monolingual. But pool is first and foremost pool. Although pool is practically destroyable, pool is ultimate. Pool non-deconstructable. Yet pool came before everything else. There was the pool and the pool was pool. Pool *is sous rature*. Pool is its own absolute reflection. Pool is the absolute polis you, no matter what, enter. Pool is syllogism. Pool contra logical. But pool pro thinking. Ergo pool is ultimately good (for you). Where pool begins pool is already over. Pool is where you only have to make one right or wrong step. Where the pool ends the word begins and where it begins beginning *un*ends. Pool deafness, pool languagelessness. Underwater a wrist watch goes off. Did you hear that? And off again.

## Melancholy Swimmer

And dawn wouldn't come till dawn when the non-swimmer, the permanently dehydrated simulacrum swimmer, the would-be swimmer, pale-skinned, quasi-invisible, turns up in our summer sleep at the focus of polis' civic space for silent thinking and begins to write down what thinking *is*. And the thinking thought, the knowing thought is of a melancholic past always already advancing, long-erased events one thought to be motionless and idle motioning an inch closer to where we are every time we think. Thinking that is to come is thinking of the history of *now*, an alternative thought of thinking in which the hydrophilic would never reach margins, fluidity fuses into concrete and the thinking thought we are thinking of remains unthought-of. Underground panorama, acropolis sky. The pool, the thinking place in which the hydrophilic would see cyclops underwater and thinking, reaching the bottom of the pool, bounces back to the initial thought with which it began thinking of anything at all. For now thinking in the world is always already and only pool. Pool *emptiful*. Liquefaction holds no idiosyncratic thought, o water, unthinking materia prima. Above the pool hefty bodies of noisy mating gulls... But, look, silent correspondent *sans* soul, didn't Barthes blame the absence of the thoughtful on love's deceptive grammar, on the overflow of body fluids which suffocate thought that is: a syntax so dense in thinking lack that thinking itself turns im*passible*? O the apathetic thought. Where thinking fails thinking the impossible. Didn't Nietzsche blame it on the fall of tragedy? *I* blames it on soulless motel rooms of the necropolis. The unthinkable height of heliopolis. The anonymous author blames it on the artificial quotas between history's unbearable/bare estates. Look, thoughtless reader, Hans Castorp's sickness is self-inflicted. Stachura's Janek Pradera in *Axing* walks off one night into a winter storm. Buchner's Lenz disappears in the Alps for good. Benjamin confronts the cyclop in a hotel room in the Catalan town of Portbou. Attila József meets the minotaur in the maze of the South Danubian rail route, a

frosty December evening in 1937 (although when I say
frosty, I don't mean to sound emotive; I mean that the night
was extremely cold). Woolf meets the medusa deep under the
River Ouse. Radnóti's nightmare, deprived of any human
thought (while the roar of canons rolls from Bulgaria) begins
in the hills of Serbia and ends in Western Hungary near the
Austrian border on the outskirts of the village of Abda. He
insists on holding on to his notebook along the last journey.
The Bridge Man's monster manifests itself in a gunshot to his
head after he leaves the Goergen Asylum of Döbling.
Rockenbauer, the diver, faces *it* at the foot of Naszály in a
small orchard with chestnut trees. The new born calf escaped
this kind of end but only because Anna was there to dive after
her in one of the offshoots of the River Cam one afternoon
this spring. She swam behind the animal covered in mud and
shit and pushed her towards the riverbank with all her
strength. These exclusive cosmic events fulfilling our
antagonists' desire to lead organic life back into its inanimate
state. To put an absolute end to thought. But look, my silent
correspondent *sans* thought, melancholy swimmer, the hyper-
real swimmer, the non-swimmer insists. And it insists on
thinking of a thinking which can endure its own thought.
Early winter was already cold that year, temperature falling
under zero. Two trucks rolled in to the factory yard early
morning, as early as six am. Both pigs were transported from
one of the best home-farms of the Eastern country. And the
feast soon would begin. Imagining or remembering the busy
scene from Brueghel's memoir may help, if not more
accurate than one's own recollections. The dismantling of the
bodies, a Renaissance medical atlas, rigorous anatomic
precision; the aesthetics of slaughter a posteriori. Then
thought, the secondary. The meticulous tip-toeing of a small
group of men and women. The industrious self-involvement.
Not one left without a job (and *I* is the one hiding in the
bathroom covering ears, nose, eyes and mouth). Bile, flesh,
burning fur, the carcass. Intestines stripped by drawing them
through fists. Stained concrete and ice. It was winter
everywhere. This winter for me was always already blood.
There is no real difference, the dead poet claims in her
notebook on twentieth-century poetics posthumously found

in her Buda apartment left behind, between perpetrator and its subject; they take it in turns over the history of grammar. Because there are places, they say, whose function as *place* is transparent, a transparency always already controversial, like contourless water in the public pool, or the vacuum of thoughtless thinking as if they have been travelling through various temporary addresses through a tim*eless* atlas of the emptied out human mind. My patient correspondent *sans* words, I woke and the sky was painted purple illuminating the house opposite, a lighthouse in the dark, in an otherworldly light. It looked as if the building had been derelict for many years, almost haunted. And as if the traveller, who has just woken up, would have just arrived all at once at the house he had been searching for all his life. Post Scriptum. A badger crossed the road in the city centre in Sheffield a few metres in front of me as I was cycling to the pool this morning. The one you have been to, with yellow and black stripes. Before it crossed, it would look both ways, as if to see if cars were coming. Then vanished quickly in a stranger's garden whose name I do not know. I saw the badger later drawn on an information board for walkers in the woods. It became the *schema* of itself which explained its structure and anatomy. A secretive mammal, the encyclopaedia also said. So should this book be about defining love? A letter in which *I* will want to write in a discursive manner as if *I* were really typing it to you. And a kind of typing which is meant to be performed with an alternative affection? The type of love W. S. Graham paints into words in his letters to Peter Lanyon, or the kind Denise breathes into poems to a dead son. The love Cézanne injects into apples. And at this point of the eulogy I can hear you say I am contradicting myself yet again. And that this paradox is insufferable for you. But would you accept your role and become my dead reader following the manic edits of the faithful typist, always already seated whose name, we don't know why, but we don't know, the letter writer's meta-hieroglyphs, the public servant's self-reflexive Gardiner sign Y3s (whereby one should imagine the symbol of a scribe's ink-mixing palette, a vertical case to hold writing reeds, and a leather pouch to hold the black and red ink blocks), disputations about summer and winter pool, his dreamy doodles on amoraphobia, long-spun debates between bird and fish. Would you, nameless lover? Without fleeing to the edge of Holkham Bay? Always already no further, as we live on an island and because beyond that only the sea and the North Pole. Without reacting or interrupting? Post Scriptum 2. Yet could all this be a poor aporia lacking scribal thought and cursive tradition, a thinking lack, a bottomless discourse *ad nauseam. Ad vitam aeternam. Ad* drowning? For where the pool ends, the body begins and where cold concrete dominates, the warm ink tiled sky fades. Post Scriptum 3. There is a tiny Norwegian island in the Oslo Fjord, a former children's prison from which once a boy attempted to escape. He'd been sent there for killing a whale. But of course we all know that the boy was the whale. That the story is merely allegory. He ran across the frozen fjord to reach the mainland but fell into an ice gap and submerged. And it's because water consists of nothing other than intuition. A life instinct; as if somehow you could conquer weight and ignore the decadent *bar* (p 2.45 p /bar= F/A, the ratio of force on the area over which that force is distributed) on your skin that, as if it were lead, drags your body downwards.

**Enunciation**

*The Rhetorical Swimmer*

Enunciation continues in the Libyan Desert, the letter begins. It continues in order to solidify time. Imagine the size of the Sahara as an enormous pool. Visualise the various types of swimmers in the linear *now*. The monochromic cave in which Heidegger, hiding, while a storm's raging outside, compares the act of swimming to the paradox of writing. Examine the staff at the pool, the instructors, the objects, painted into words, inhabiting liquefied space, the industry of clothing the body in water, their rapid alterations from bathing suit to frogmen's costume, from silky skin to nudity: the speed of metamorphoses of the body in motion, the race of the thinking metaphor. As if we had been improvising writing all along and presented the poem as slip of the tongue *ex abrupto*, an involuntary lapse, language *ad absurdum*. In the work *Nilling*, rhythm, the wondering flâneur, flows freely, without punctuation, *sans* full stops, it flows as artless metaphor, always already morphing into another shell, a morphology which opposes premeditation or destination. No etymology can reveal the origin of word. So far history failed to find the absolute thought. A history full of dead tropes and fish. Have you thought of this before? To be able to speak of swimming one must *un*speak the original text, conquer cultural cyclops underwater, undo Odyssey's amnesia, erase Beowulf's psyche. O gullible Gilgamesh, curious Kalevala, the big bubble of Babel, the polyglot water globe *sans* love. Anthropology, arrhythmic rhythm of the surviving universal self *sans* sadness. History, *figura etimologica* with other words, the amphora body, the swimmer, in which blood turns into

bone. Archaeology, the swimmer's slim figurine
into dead language, solid *metaphora*. One must
resist an end by this resistance. One must go with
the necessary flow. The writing body, the semi-
absent, the figuratively dead pen, the elastic *I* with
fine physique and soft weight in water motions
towards being. Did you know that Nikolaus
Wynnman is the first one to write about the hazard
of drowning? Passages in the Latin *Colymbetes*
suggest that one should use air-filled cow bladder
to stay on the surface of the water and imitate
animals (o Jean-Jacques, o Crusoe, o Tarzan) to be
able to swim to and fro in the enclosed garden in
order to survive on the page. And despite it all, the
poem flows with the flow. But how should we
break out a revolution in the writing space when
the soul, the script is stuck between time's
invisible margins, how to find the new language
we could speak with everyone and everywhere.
How can the soul *sans* soul, the anchor, save the
body from drowning? At the bottom of the pool an
old language invents time. Original language
announces its origin. The daring thought that dares
you dive down to the bottom of the pool covered
with dry leaves, human hair and skin and return
with nothing but a handful of dry leaves, human
hair and skin. O rhetorical reader; live a good
life, sing a long song, die a quiet death.

*The Museologist Swimmer*

And drifting into winter, my hydrophilic friend, on
a clear blue sky day when pools politicize thought,
the aquatic flâneur's thinking day, the drowning
day, the daring, on the feast day of theophany, o
Ponderosa Parks, when the fish, even caymans,
feel somewhat epiphanic, feeling or desiring
something that might resemble *desire* or *feeling*,
the feeling, thinking day when we consecrate the

four walls of the pool, Adam and I were strolling
down West Street in search of a new home for him
while passing by Glossop Road Baths, an authentic
Turkish Bath, half of which morphed by now into
Wetherspoons. And it is when the counting began.
A moment when enunciation enounces itself as
calculation. Have you noticed how we begin to
estimate heights when we reach the bottom of a
civic space? How we catalogue love, the living and
the dead and rearrange alphabets, infinite numbers,
swimming pools and baths that once existed in
polis' thinking place. The catharsis of melancholic
archives, their cosmic clutter, the data. As dry as
bones. Attercliffe Baths 1879 to 1981, Corporation
Street 1879 to 1962, Upperthorpe 1896 to present,
Glossop Road, Ladies 1898 to 1991, Brightside
1899 to 1964, Park 1899 to 1989, Heeley 1909 to
present, Rivelin Valley 1909 to 1939, Hillsborough
1929 to 1991, Concord from date unknown to date
unknown, Graves 1991 to present, King Edwards
Swimming Pool 1936 to present, Springs 1950 to
date unknown, Sheaf Valley 1972 to 1991, by now
demolished, altered, redefined as other,
readdressed as absent, liminal, departed; the city
dweller calls these departures *cul-de-sac*, with lots
of question marks graffitied on the ginnels. Our
swimmer *sans* soul identifies new addresses as loss
for loss's sake. Loss's sign, the swimmer says, is
parenthesis *sans* oxygen, *sans* breath. Loss is also
metamorphing multi-function of local public baths.
And meaning, always already morphing into loss,
embraces error. O silent reader, the other day,
strolling in the middle of summer, I misread the
outer signs on one of the many swimming pools in
Budapest. *Gőz*, the element that carries the
grapheme of liquid, the sound of water-particles,
the lexicon says, is what constitutes a *steam* room.
The other word, the spectral, its eerie centre held
together by a bass vowel, is made of lethal *gáz*.
The phonetic slippage on 'Rácz Spa' fills the

aquatic flâneur with unnameable terror, even though the slippage is purely cultural, melancholic, is what one means, always already an approaching threat of the past, a slip of the thought of the swimmer self. Slippage of the phoneme is history, the dark Danube, the non-Danube, the simulacrum soul that runs through the continent of time always already as flimsy figure of speech, always already as a water corpse. The following day I found a random note by someone called Martin in the Sheffield archive. Martin was currently doing his family tree when he bumped into his grandmother's name in the local records. According to the obituary the cause of death was suicide by drowning in Bathing Pool, that's long vanished from the map by now with grandma's water corpse, in Endcliffe Park, that's still there with you drifting across the lawn wondering about Martin in the museum *et cetera*. Or take the antiheroine of the 19th century ballad, solitary swimmer, the melancholic Central European femme fatale who, unhusbanded by the murder of her lawful husband, the plot executed by the deadly duo, Agnes and her amorous inamorato, is destined to wash her tunic, the garment for the body, in the flux of the riverwater *ad infinitum*. The murkiness of the ballad, the quiet catharses of small archives, catastrophe composed from misread city signs, the soul's shameful symbols, that mistake we make misprinting alphabets that turn pool's public health care, that cleanses the city, to homicide, that erases it. Glossic guilt creeps in on us. Eureka. Eureka. Guilt creeps in on us. It is with density. Did you know? The falling apple and the orbiting moon are both pulled by the same force.

## The Polyglot Swimmer

And it is the moment when we accelerate. And so what if we were to imagine the pool as a Ballardian swim-race, the poem as an Olympiad organised on the M25 with multi-laned motorways where each driver, like the old pensioner, the swimmer in the Budapest bath, resembling a World War I pilot in the middle of imagined air-raids, swims in old fashioned goggles and helmets, each in the globe-shaped realm of their thoughts, thinking of a life versed in many satire versions, being-or-speeding-in-the-world. Certain pool water allows us to swim faster than in others; it allows you to swim misleadingly too fast. It's the consistency of water. Ozone and oxygen make it almost buoyant. Then the anxiety of one's pace sandwiched between two speeding bodies in the lane. Imagine fatalities, brutalities, strokes in the middle of the flip turn, limbs occasionally entangling the other's during performing free style. The comic sluggishness of heavy cargo overtaking heavy cargo; camions accelerating already at the point of departure. Once I spotted a video snapshot posted on a public portal to the world by a grieving mother from Norfolk. The fast-moving film featured the son's motorbike journey en route to Norwich from Kings Lynn, camera attached to his helmet all along. So is it, silent speeder, the closest, perhaps, you could ever get to the finale. Is this the split second of thought's absolute exit. Then picture the poem as Sebald's skull. To the skull a camera attached when his car crashes with a lorry in Poringland on the Lowestoft Road in the midst of his East Anglian mindscape. Sometimes isn't it the body which saves the soul from drowning? The polyglot swimmer always swims in a parallel text. And so expression begins in order to capture absence. It is to capture the gap in difference between now and now. It begins, the letter continues, about ten thousand years ago in the

Libyan Desert carved into the Gilf Kebir Plateau. It begins with a speaking alter ego, the anonymous Count the discoverer, the polyglot, the multilingual camouflage spy with webbed feet, the political centaur, pro-Habsburg and pro-British, the German empathiser, and Russian sympathiser, super-real paneuropean amphibian who, according to Mrs Howards' article in The New York Times, if he were to be on any side, in other words, if he existed, he would be entirely on the eccentric, the one *ab origine*, that one that can't exist, the drifting archaeologist with multiple lives who in a silent documentary film, appears giraffe-like with a slight stoop and a very long nose, the controversial Count with multiple (dead) souls. So imagine this giraffe-man in his real life, in the desert one day spotted in one of the three hidden valleys of Zerzura, the Oasis of Birds he travelled to with three Britons on a De Havilland Gypsy Moth aeroplane in 1933. In this valley he explores anonymous Neolithic pictographs painted on walls of hidden caves which later he writes about in *The Unknown Sahara*. He argues that the paintings portray people attempting to rehearse breast strokes the first time in the history of art, or some ritualistic act of swimming movements, he wasn't sure. He, the anonymous author, the multi-masked, multi-scripting scribe, the pseudo-scientist, explains that the mystery around the cave is to do with climate change, a theory so radical, so *ahead of time*, that it had to be omitted from the book. But, dear editor, isn't it the emission of the past that composes our problem poem *now*; always already catching up with the writing in the present? Figures, swimming up and down and to and fro in the pictograph, floating, drifting, relaxed, as if always already drifting towards eventuality in a neon-lit public spa. Slowly. Slowly. Moving away. Moving away towards probability, propelled towards the meaning lack. Consider absence as the archetype of all future poems. O empty Ladybower Reservoir.

Speaking of a pool shrinks the Earth. Earths normally end by water. Laminate the book. This I know. But I am curious to know too, what you know. My silent correspondent, tell me what you think. Post Scriptum. This summer's last swim took place in the Old Buda pool late August. I was finishing my usual lengths when through the steamed-up goggles I noticed something floating on the surface of the water. I swam a stroke closer and I saw the first bronze leaf of the autumn. Then I saw the body of *lepke*, the lepidopteran, the anonymous no chance butterfly. It was, though, flimsier. Thinner than absence. Thinner than poem. Diluted. A shaft of otherworldly light. Dear aquatic archaeologist. I was following a stranger's post on a social portal all summer. Her messages contained images of recreation works that took place in her enclosed garden lasting many months; part of which was to remove the old swimming pool situated in its centre. The blue tiled abyss, deprived of blue tiles, deconstructed, filled up with soil, drowning in *itself*, eventually morphed into ideal lawn. And we, the world, witnessed the metamorphosis, the relentless works lasting all summer, the filmic series of radical concretisation of a once fluid milieu, *un*seeing that the swimming pool, which had just been erased before the billion eyes, the original, the swimming pool a priori, the parallel pool, parallel to pool, no matter what but will have been there all along from the very beginning.

**Rockenbauer, the Diver**

We are, the anonymous author writes, right in the middle of the conversation. But where do we go from the centre if the movement on the page is always vertical. That is to say if one is always already determined to move away from oneself, in other words, one is also always bound to descend. What I mean is what choice do you have? Other than gently waving the poem, the body, the object, hand-made, hermetic, off as a silent witness watching it disappearing into itself? It's great as it could be worse, she also adds. And (if everyone leaves in the end, look, a small silver Volkswagen fading slowly into nowhere) so is the submersion (don't you think, as if one perpetually felt rushed to write; as if always already running out of language – or running out of love –, moving against the living speed, between writing contra writing within the given timespace event, the point of departure and the point of disappearance – the point of disappointment); so here and now we *un*choose immersion into the study of hydrostatics, as temporary readers of science of fluid under pressure. Look. Rockenbauer's dip should be globally, in fact, cosmically, renowned (o sea-sick lover, don't be captivated by climax and forget to remember to follow up the thread of narratives. Those drowned children are still waiting to be rescued at the bottom of the sea) in order to find correlations between two poles of our global paradox, resolution within the irresolvable physical, fluid distance conflicting public bodies, private continents. So let us for a moment commemorate the elastic diver. The vertical writer, the sinking pen. The gravity explorer. The expeditionist *I*. The diving self. Sinking bewilder'd 'mid the dreary sea. The *I*'s global plummet into the poet's lifelong mourning of horizontality, o history of desire, o magna water. Let us remember grief. One's right to lament the lost momentum, the drowning boy, the inner Leander toiling to his death so that the silent poem, the dead poem, the dormant poem can be shaken up. But look, this parabola makes it impossible to write the book in the end. Or even to type it to you. At times it feels as if we were always already diving in this page-long, single breath exercise. At times like this the diving pool becomes Rockenbauer's fatal flânerie. Dear unfree reader. Kosztolányi's Europe too tilted head down in the Adriatic in his short reflections sketched between 1906 and 1913 travelling around the old continent through invisible cities in the Balkans down in the South of the Danubian Delta. Almost a hundred years later, Rockenbauer, the diver, ventures off to explore borders of the body in the Cuban sea. He is a documentary maker so his job is to document the underworld as aesthetically and as artlessly as it is possible.

The documentary, subtitled 'Buzos Hungaros en Aguas Cubanas' was filmed in Hawaii by the Jacques Cousteau Divers' Group in 1984 named after the oceanographer, the author of *Silent World*, the first one to dive down to the bottom of coral beds in a self-built yellow submarine. The old photo you are looking at shows the expedition group spending long days in vacuum chambers for weeks before the trip in order to train the lungs. To practise an alternative kind of breathing. A new *modus vivendi*. A simultaneous diachronic and synchronic writing exercise against time. In this continuum we all long to find, Emese the swimming instructor said in the autumn, there is infinite harmony between racing objects. You kind of adapt to the speed of the other swimming ahead or behind until there is only one single body swimming in the pool.

And so the film discusses pressure. The pressure which of course increases as one, carrying cameras, subsides. Pressure which at the moment of diving is 2.45 p (bar= F/A, that is the ratio of force on the area over which that force is distributed) on the surface of every square centimetre of the skin and 250.000 Pascal heavier than in air. And so the diving self weighs two and a half kilograms more than the landlocked poem. Another orphic paradox in itself for doesn't writing (*feeling*) feel much lighter when in water than on earth. The trip, funded by Rockenbauer's Latin American friends, was to commemorate Cousteau, the brother of Thanatos, the lover of oceanic depths, the inventor of the great diving saucer. These coral reefs had not quite been touched like *this* before. This is the way forward to swim to corals in chlorine-free water. So diving, silent witness. Let all divers of the globe unite. Viva divine sea. In which we, watchers from another world, can take a closer look at *this* one. The spectral self protected by a diving garment crawling on cameras and corals. Complicated beauty. Blonde vegetation. Soft medusa flora. A face that launch'd a thousand ships. And burnt topless towers. Look Ἑλένη. Since you always wondered. It says. We are always left with the *nulla* poem. Torture. Torturing. A torch faced down on canvas. A *no thing* like a private gesture we now lay down on sea bed. In this poem, now in darkness, the documentary maker floats in front of you on the screen, light figure, heavy diver's suit, he is surrounded by symbols and metaphora, he says. Perhaps what the foreign Buzos found in the 25m depth under sea level was more than just the corals. They met other divers of their own floating *super* self. I am unsure. Dear sinking listener, the correlation here remains unsolidified, the hiatus filled with pressure between air and aqua. The question always already rhetorical: what did the anonymous diver say to you breathing inaudible bubbles through an atmospheric skin. O horrid dream. On Sunday, Natalia Molchanova, the letter ends, in her favourite purple wet suit, drowned. The news says it was her deepest dive. The skies were clear. And there was a light breeze on the Balearic Sea.

## The *Mother*

Dear logophilic friend, collector of letters, the lepidopterist continues in another half-composed epistole, despite its mistake of being in the wrong place, gathering the wrong things, tumbling towards the wrong source of enlightenment, the poem today shows, unmistakably, a strong tendency to fall towards silence. Propelled towards the pool. Is any man wiser than Socrates or Celan sat in lotus pose wordless at opposite ends writing in air or water, the rhetorical question we might ask, one writing at the dawn, the other at the closure of writing against writing. O the absolute rhetoric of the anti-scribe. The poem, their message says, no matter how murky, should be as transparent as the pool. Composing letters, Nabokov, the philatelist claims, is a blend of dejection and high spirits, a torture and a pastime. On the other hand, he who loathes writing writing down longs for a new career as a guardian of dead moths, unsent postcards, coralised butterflies. He longs to be a museum attendant, a three-headed, multi-souled hellhound who guards an entrance no-one ever enters in fallen Saint Petersburg or clandestine Prague for a lifetime or for as long as the museum is open, in other words until it shuts. Therefore I too must, o mottephilic friend, seek the core of the fear of my other, o wing-phobia, o fluttering lover, do not write on the body of the butterfly. Knowledge of any thing that partakes in being may help ease our fear of the things it fears. Meditation or other structured breathing exercise. And you, breathless beginner of fearing, you must free your dead moth, the no chance moth struggling on glass. The estranged, furry self agonising on the border between inside and outside. Dear X, enframer of the world. A being is a being that is being. There is no simpler mediator between the moth and nothing than nothing. The moth thinks we can't see what it is being because it does not belong either to the frame, the world, or to you. No absolute pen that could navigate the poem in the writing exercise. At the bottom of this swimming pool you won't find any pre-meditated, painted lines. The body, in here lost, we could almost think, is free. And the poem continues to be never found. For what is found is already misplaced. And there we

were, remember, at the edge of the pool amongst bronze
figures illuminated in an imagined source of light, unsure
whether at the beginning or at the end of what was to take
place in between. And to pass the waiting time we were talking
of a melancholic mother all summer – her terror of talking of her
terror of talking. It is a bit like, she says in the end, when
Panna the sheepdog died. The day she became tongue-tied. The
tumour chewing a bit of her body away each day advancing a
day closer to what by now is far too far. The growth, then,
although invisible to the eye, we knew, existed because the dog
does not exist anymore. In a dog's invisible life the speed of
gnawing, the unnoticed non-being gnaws seven times swifter.
O phlegmatic old dog. There is another dog seven times faster
than the dog inside the dog inside. And we were there again at
the edge of the pool to understand the speed of time seven
times speedier, the speed of sadness speeding seven times
faster. Dear gatherer, we frame the world so it can be seen or
understood or found. And we saw that it was already autumn, a
liminal season. The pool was not quite yet escaping its own
momentum, in there time was seven times slower than real
time, seven times idler, I thought in the sauna, because I *was*
there at the edge of the melancholic pool. And I saw my
reflections on the glass. And through the glass I watched
bronze bodies swimming up and down to and froing between
two tiled walls like trafficking dark tree logs, o all the Y-shaped
non-swimmers floating down the dark Danube. Multiple and
simultaneous realities of pool-water. Dear fictitious friend,
Ottlik thinks we who partake in being in the real world can
imagine this world always already unreal. Being non-being, in
other words. He imagines his protagonists to be invisible to
others. So he spends most of his time in an imaginary pool
thinking he too is unseen. But in a pool clarity, in a pool
enlightenment and transparency pool's always static and
already idle no matter how fast you swim. There is another
poem seven times faster inside the poem inside. And in the
pool another pool. The same pool. In this pool the poem is a
poem unmoving *you*. Dear unmoved Y. A blue tiled concrete
basin filled with chlorine and water is the same tiled and
concrete basin filled with chlorine and water you bathed in the
other day, no matter what David Hockney says. And it is where
we stood at the edge of the season with bronze bodies

illuminated in otherwordly light. There were no warning signs to warn us but the pool. Despite loud loudspeakers urging swimmers to get out of the water, you, madam, as well, in the pink swim cap, sir, in stripy trunks, the rules apply to you too. A light summer storm came with muffled thunder and Y shaped lightning above the water. And we had to leave the pool that, despite the disruptions, remained the same. And with us the bus meandered across Water Town, the old Buda district in the summer storm that wouldn't soften or ease down. Soon cones and conkers were falling on the roof, each minute stronger and louder until we thought war must make this sound. Outside the summer streets were white, flooded with thick ice, hailstones the size of cherries or pomegranates. Contours of the world melted, blurred as if this world were the extension of the pool. A water world in which everything could become everything else. And at this border crossing of beings the city became a river, as if the city had always been this river or more precisely as if the city had never existed before and after the flood, and in this river city the cars and the trams had to learn to drive on. There's another city seven times faster in the city inside. And then the outside became invisible. And inside utterly silent. Needless to say the metamorphosis didn't last longer than a quarter of an hour, almost as long as it takes to narrate it all to you, a quarter of an hour where I knew I belonged. Then the sun shone, the sky turned blue and the city continued to navigate on. Dear visible other, now imagine the terror of an imagined mother floating somewhere in the middle of events, the dying sheepdog, the moth on the glass, the bus that was drowning, writing contra writing and lovers of words against love, remember the hail storm, like an erasure that can turn the city into ice. The night butterfly, that agonises in another language. Dead moths who can reinvent their lives in this one. O loather of lexis. We stood there at the edge of the pool talking of sleepless nights we spent with shutters shut. The collective fear of night apparitions, the triangular dark body on our white walls. The fan-shaped fear's night visit. The bizarre genus camouflaged on the black window-glass. Body flattened, as if it could make us think it were only glass. As if it were darkness. Unbelonging to the world or to you. Dear moth-fearer. Overcome your fear and be a mother, an Aurelian, the bronze-bodied swimmer, golden, like the colour of chrysalis or the drooling sun in sunset. A collector of *lepke*, a day or night time butterfly in my mother's tongue. Dear museophile friend, collector of clutter. Everyone collects pools in the end. But in their centre all pools have a plug through which they regularly escape. To overcome the obsession we must suspend the writing it all down. Walk, or write, like *lepke* on the surface of rough terrains, Ottlik reasons, without clothes, barefoot amongst thorn bushes and gigantic water melons. Moths are bizarre creatures, Woolf, the moth-murderer writes in her essay on the plane back to England at the end of one summer, her aircraft tossed around in turmoil. Sebald, the moth mourner, encounters it in his grotty B&B room on the East Anglian shoreline. They have, he claims, an angular relationship to a bright celestial light such as the Moon. But those celestial objects are so far away, that even after travelling great distances the change in angle between the moth and the light source is negligible. In other words they think the lamp, towards which they come plummeting downwards in a spiral flight, is the Moon. There is no right word to change the mind of the lost genus, to explain that they are mistaken, that they made a fatal navigational error. Their innate longing for both darkness and light. The moth, of course, is the poem. And the poem, of course is a swimmer in the pool doing front crawl. Head facing down towards the tiled bottom. Head turning skywards when out for a breath. The alternating arms' rolling movement, the experts say, prepare the body for an easier recovery compared to butterfly. Dear longing writer. Adam thinks moth is a sign of writing flowing smoothly. The room is a room in another room. Imago moulting into imago waiting to become. Dear Adam. The old photograph you sent me with the image of the Underwater Swimmer was taken in a Budapest pool in 1917. Swimmer Underwater, the dormant swimmer waiting to be woken from 1978, which I came across much later, seems to be to me the perfect reflection of its model; Hockney's version of the swimmer perhaps somewhat lighter or darker than its prototype; however, in both, spiky reflections strike the water in electric bolts of light as their swimmers glide, curious creatures, disembodied crab claws, the online photo albums guide the eye. Or perhaps like headless Rilke

torsos. Only the striped trunks ensure us the body of
Underwater Swimmer is human as the head disappears in the
movement of the water. It casts a deep shadow of Swimmer
Underwater, the dormant swimmer waiting to be woken on the
shallow bottom, while other tiny shadows melt into the fluid
scene, circling his body like newly hatched tadpoles, orbiting
around its miniature self. In the split-second exposure, the
swimmer's extended body seems to hover suspended in the
water. A floating faun. Contours of a fluid angel drawn from
violin strings. Shooting a horizontal skywards. Distancing.
Distancing. Slowly. Slowly. Away from itself. A melancholy
tulip. But at what point does meaning become distortion. There
is meaning inside inside. Dear liminal moth on the glass.
Márai, the headless author, unseen and unheard of, in his
studies on Turkish spas of old Buda districts sketched in the
1940s, argues that humanity can only sustain itself if it steps
out of history. It must swim out of its old shell. The dark
Danube. To exist you must exit, he adds in the notebook, at
which stage he's still living in the country not having quite left,
beheaded or bereft of love yet, nor deprived of the accent on
his laurel crown, by then peripatetically cocooned in the coat of
another writer in a country that does not recognise or see him.
His overnight train at this stage of the narrative had not yet
crossed any visible border. He, the invisible prophet in exile
inside and outside, thinks; the wise perform aquatic thinking in
the inner domes of steam rooms away from the public. For the
hooded writer the spa is an aquatic monastery for fluid
thinking. The fools, he reiterates, exposed to the world, scorch
their skin outdoors in the midday sun. In the milieu of
indifference, the anonymous author adds, for the self to survive
you must write to a reader always already dead. Dear composer
of chaos. At what point does distortion remain beautiful. At
what point is origin original? Where did we begin this actual
discourse? And at what point of our loving it does the body, the
poem, the thing, the subject of our affection and attention
become hideous or repulsive? Socrates thinks it is when a thing
becomes unhidden, that is, found. Dear terror-ridden reader, we
must hope this book is not going to terrorise anyone. Look,
worshipper of blue sky and sun. We know that moths will burn
their wings, which proves that light is good for them, or else
they had flown not, where they agonise, the poem within the

poem says. The source of light, a Tungsram light bulb with
filament made from tungsten instead of carbon. The inscription
reads '1910: wire lamp with a drawn wire and a light
indestructible'. The globe, the old advert adds, is as small as
the bulb. The bulb as great as the globe, is what they mean.
There is a globe within the bulb, is what they really think.
Talking of swimming pools shrinks the Earth. It turns the poem
into a photo essay. The narratives of terror and affection,
always turning backwards, towards darkrooms, but already
propelling towards safe neon light. The limbo between affinity
and aversion. The see-sawing: when you are up in the air I am
always already on the ground. In moments when the clouds
close in above one's skull and hooded crows begin their
necessary seasonal discourse so that one's major organs quiver.
Dear x-rayed reader. Socrates, sat still, in a pupa-position at the
margin thinks, we don't need to laminate the globe. Stay in
darkness, invisible, he reasons, do not illuminate the room.
There is a secret path of writing without a turn. Be atropos, the
moth-enthusiast, the cosmic, he says, whose mind is the Moon,
eyes the Sun. It stares skywards. It has a thousand heads and a
thousand feet like a universal insect. Be tautology; darkness
inside another darkness inside. Dear illuminator. Let there be
light inside the light. Look. Ottlik sets his protagonists in the
milieu of Lukács spa in Budapest where the two friends spend
whole days in silence. For the men, who occasionally hum or
nod, pool is a perfect place for pool and people watching, idly,
cocooned in sunshine, waiting for a freed up sunbed or
eavesdropping carefree banter about the results of the water
polo final. The unreliable narrator tells us a few pages later that
the friends say nothing because at the time they thought of
nothing else except nothing. Except the anchor of a lost ship at
Trieste Bay. Near the bay is Rilke's dark and lonely castle.
Dear numb child the child inside the numb. In the novel's
public pool the two protagonists of course eventually speak.
The subject is a manuscript a dead friend had left behind. What
hope do we have left, the dead friend reasons on the page, if
not even a mother can read writing without writing. O lost
moth-finder. Don't break me, the moth says: my head is made
of glass. Can you see what I am thinking? Or perhaps it says:
can you see what I am.

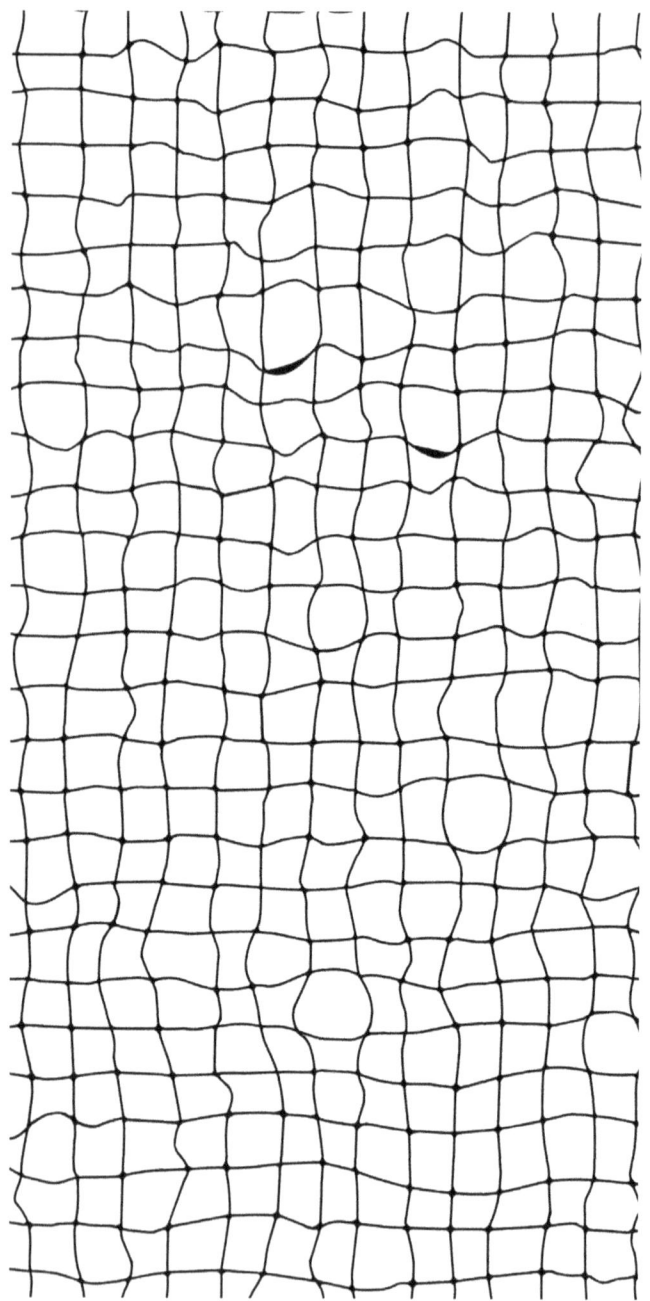

*Book Two*

**Pool Epitaphs and Other Love Letters**

[Postcard 2]

What does your wordless absence say.
Who were they for, those promises.
Nothing was true, if now all's gone
though it was – wasn't it – serious.


Hopes, denied, recoil to stiffen
like glazed weeds tangled under ice.
Time does not always heal the damage
but tamps it down then seals it tight.


Ears and mouths must close on quiet
whose patient night gapes in appeal.
Willed silence is a short-lived luxury.
Speak as you can & while I still can hear.

Denise Riley, 'Time How Short'

[† *Prologos:* [*Apostil 1* / *Illuminations 1*]; I:1] *'And so when we enter the swimming pool'*

And so when we enter the swimming pool in the middle of summer, the patient concierge continued guiding us through semi-lit corridors to the swimming pool, let's continue to be patient, since today's swim is another attempt to do it well on the page. To navigate the body home through language. To home in on the world. Another attempt to do it wrong again for being in water has its own paradox. When you *are* in pool you are *not*, in other words. Because the anti-swimmer exists and it insists on swimming, swimming against the *right* direction. The self-doubter who, on behalf of us would doubt ourselves, the erratic eraser who scraps every second thought before we could feel, desire, think or write it down. The anti-scribe in the faithful scribe who writes a poem to parallel the poem you write. Because there is always an anti-lover inside the lover inside. A twin writer resisting writing writing down. An absent swimmer self always already swimming opposite the necessary tide contradicting anything we attempt to understand and so disputing the *thing* we love. A poem counterpart inside the poem outside, a parasite poem gnawing the poem from inside making its way towards the outside. But my dear parallel scribe, the scribe inside the patient scribe continued, despite this hooded figure, this apathetic apparition always appearing at the edge of the pool, the marginal anti-swimmer, the phantom counteractor, the drowning instructor, one must move the body across the horizon as if one's (eternal) life were at stake... .

**[Pool Epitaph i; letter I:13] '...And so on a hot August day'**


...And so on a hot August day, on a feeling, thinking day, on a sublime swimming day, on the *chance* day, the brave day, when the swimmer knows that on such a day anything could happen, after much anxious anticipation we arrived at the swimming pool and saw that *it* wasn't *there*. More precisely we did not see that it was there. In other words, the local pool in the heart of the XI district normally perched on one of the gentle slopes of the Buda Hills was gone, the pool was misplaced. The sign, hardly comprehensible, said: *pool isn't here* – yet, my sympathetic swimmer, how can a swimmer swim *sans* swimming pool? O pool present, pool past. And misplaced too searching for our missing pool, my patient concierge and I drifted into the middle of Hieronymus' garden of earthly disgust and delights. Imagine *this* pathological pool within *that* pathological pool. Pathological because right beneath our living swimmer a drowned swimmer is swimming too. So let's take a risk and imagine this image without doubt. It's our local swimming pool at dusk. The pool, this pool, another pool, the same pool. The playful pool. The absent pool present for now. The pondering pool, the pond full of various magic and mirage. And we entered with a body we both loathed and loved while we were alive. We entered with a body that both loathed and loved us before it drowned. Then in the blue tiled dressing room we undressed quietly. And leaving the body behind us *we* dived into Jerome's triptych. Both present and absent, as apparition there and elsewhere, we disappeared in dusk and appeared in the middle of another pool, at its focal point the musical fountain of your childhood on Margaret Island in Budapest with your small sun-tanned body wandering in water with other tiny swimmers drifting through a cryptic century at a time when time was not yet timed. The century was empty as a tomb. And we were there at the edge of the

pool and we saw that the page in front of us was always
already the only page, the same page, the same
composite of blue sky and pool. And this was the heroic
Hieronymus moment when one's phantom foot slips
on the tiles and our silhouettes took off...

[*PE ii; letter II:13*] '*...Dear silent swimmer sans silhouette*'

...Dear silent swimmer *sans* silhouette, *sans* soul, bon courage. These are letters from a pool long morphed into a landscape somewhere else. Let us move in the triptych playfully *in order*. Contours of the poem inside and outside concealed in dusk. Next to the pool the largest zoo in the world, as large as the world; in the large zoo the saddest animals, as sad as sky. The sky, blue tiled, as rectangular as a regular swimming pool. In this ordinary pool the drawings of exotic animals, some somewhat irregular, carefully copied from mid-15$^{th}$ century humanist scholar Cyriac of Ancona's travelogues. And we were there at the edge of the pool and we saw that the page in front of us was always already the only page, the same page, the same composite of blue sky and pool. On the surface of the water floating artlessly on its back, the Dodo read a book. Unicorns grew fins. Small fish emerged from the depth with wings. Pre-semantic *girlboy* pre-thinking, pre-feeling always already outside the sentence, picked at a giant strawberry. A porcupine, looking lost, rushed across the page. A tiny black reptile, unborn at this stage, will have gone missing on the next. Bosch's triptych, the art historian claims, is meant to be deciphered chronologically, linearly, from left to right. From dawn to dusk. From delight to disgust. By the time we left the pool it was winter outside. The speaking fountain within the fountain from childhood snowed-up. On the ice rink there was a gull skating and carving hieroglyphs the fish underneath could not read. Then our quiet concierge shut the altarpiece's shutters and the book became a crystal ball orbiting around itself in amniotic fluid. A baby seal crawled out on the margin. This water universe with the baby seal much later in 1986 turned into an installation artist's Oval Court composed in a Victorian terraced house on Beck Road in Hackney, with the baby seal morphing into the artist's manifold bodies whose original was lost among the replicas; around the photocopied self-portraits swimming up and down in an imaginary blue universe corroding fish, dead embryos preserved inside glass bottles, decomposing vegetables were floating in some repulsive jelly stuff. When you zoom in on the artist's crying faces you can see her many bodies, twisting, twitching, are in pain too. But don't you think, my scribbling, drooling navigator, that reading must take place simultaneously from left to right and right to back. Bosch's triptych pool is one and only pool, from pool the ephemeral past to pool a retro-future, from pool *fear*ful logos to pool fright*ful* lexis, from pool Eros to pool Thanatos, pool psychophobia, pool *sans* sense, *sans* philia to pool *emptiful*.

[PE iii; letter III:13] '...And the now was always already pool'

...And the now was always already pool and only pool. Pool emptiful. Help me to write these letters to fill them mind*fully* with substance. Dear Absent, dear solar swimmer, my cherished Scribe inside the scribe outside. These letters we sent had already been sent from *the* pool long gone from the nautical map. The pool was bathing in dusk on a feeling, thinking day when pool forgives body and body forgives pool. On the day when we cleanse the body for Eros in the pool. Creatures, mindlessly, were at rest on the margin of the pool: lion, elephant and giraffe. O shadows. O melancholia, o sick poem. We stood there unclothed with bodies illuminated in bright neon lights. And we looked and when we looked we felt ashamed. But, look, sinless swimmer, sunny soul, water for us was desire with no consequence. And the earth was already laminated on the surface of which the poem slipped on with our slippery *poly-histor* who narrates history of feeling and thinking *sans* desire, *sans* thought simultaneously backwards and forward, the omniscient deconstructor, the Derrida-dissector, Thomas the doubter, the anti-teacher, the *chancer*, who, long-beaked, bespectacled, slightly hunched, no longer a fish, but not yet a bird, always in-between, walking up and down and to and fro at the margin of the page in a white dressing gown, knows that he doesn't know for he only knows of now. A deserted now that deserts us too. And so, our fearless failer, the amnesiac history-teller, the anti-swimmer, the bad learner who learns that he'll never learn what's ahead, what's past, says today, on the thinking, feeling day, the chance day, the playful, he prefers not to swim. O pool semi-lit, semi-light. Apo phainesthai ta phainomena. Let what shows itself be seen from itself, just as it shows itself from itself...

[*PE iv; letter IV:13*] '...*Apo phainesthai ta phainomena*'

...Apo phainesthai ta phainomena. Let the flower turn flesh. Rainbow into meteorological data. Glorious glory into guilt or guano. Animate into inanimate. But my inanimate reader with imagination. An animal has no escape to be anything else because it has no imagination. It lives life without consequence. It desires and it desires to be alive and this, not so much feeling, but longing is its minimum consequence. And the poem inconsequentially, maximalistically yet artlessly, desires to be *creature* too. Abstractly alive, inanimate but intimate it moves discreetly as timespace event, before it turns into bone. Dear fossilised lover, but why codex the body, sex the soul, the other. Let's come close enough to keep a distance. Let's leave the book semi-shut. But this frustration, this quiet fury between delight and disgust, the split second between feeling and failing body (or the heart or the catastrophic poem), this coming too close to keep a distance, this historic hesitation that neutralises the composer and nullifies the composed before accident or mercy would compose it into composition, this meticulous tip-toeing over miniatures, the trivia, the frivolous details of arranging and deranging, the pause at semi-turning the page, nevertheless is always also fuelled by affection even if the creature we are fond of wears the medusa's head. The attentive artist, my grammarphobic reader, calls it *making love* [from *lufo*, *lufu*, or *luuu*]. Responsiveness, in other words, with which we observe the body, while alive, just before it turns. Before dusk sets in the civic swimming space. The painter for this purpose, then, Vasari writes in 1568 in *Vita di Leonardo*, carries to a room of his own into which no one entered save himself alone, lizards great and small, crickets, serpents, butterflies, grasshoppers, bats, and other strange kinds of suchlike animals (some of these animals he dissected), out of

the number of which [...] he formed a great ugly
creature, most horrible and terrifying, which emitted a
poisonous breath and turned the air to flame; and he
made it coming out of a dark and jagged rock,
belching forth venom from its open throat, fire from
its eyes, and smoke from its nostrils, in so strange a
fashion that it appeared altogether a monstrous and
horrible thing; and so long did he labour over making
it, that the stench of the dead animals in that room was
past bearing, but the artist did not notice it, so great
was the love that he bore towards art. But algophobic,
ergophobic lover, so great is the artist's love that he
gives his life for what for us is only a word-item in the
dull catalogue of common things. For us, o sceptic
spectator, this artless sacrifice is too artful and almost
as histrionic as the history of swimming. And so great
was the scribe's compassion for the master that he
became his witness, his confidante, his companion co-
composing the monstrosity made from ecstasy,
excrement and chance. Viva Vasari. Viva *post*-script
survivor. And viva all faithful anonymous scribes who
love with the wrong love.

[*PE v; letter V:13*] *'For the poem is grotesque'*

For the poem is grotesque. *My* awful body, once in heaven, today, on a feeling, thinking day, on a chance day patroned by mercy and coincidence, is as hideous as any body in the compendium of beasts, active, being, alive. The chance body, as if always in-between before and after it metamorphs. Flower into flesh. Hiatus into horror. Bestial into sublime. Wait. Don't go, concierge. Don't come too near. Commiserate the repulsive poem in the poem. The pathological inside the fit. Because looking at it from a non-poetic perspective, the dead poet writes in her notebook found in her Buda apartment post mortem, this so called thing, this phantom phenomenon, is bizarre, and even more so today. My curious critic. Cryptic scriptor. Post-scriptum collector. Let's come a little closer to keep a distance, the posthumous poet writes. Here lies the poem, the cyber warrior, the solar swimmer, the mutilated messenger, signalling, flaunting, stammering the news in this, that and any other way she can – everything that she has seen and is capable of, telling us that she has indeed been where she has been.

[*PE vi; letter VI:13*] '...*Viva carcass*'

...Viva carcass. By the time these pool monologues are available in print, the anonymous scribe writes, spending his entire life in the half-finished house of being, my faithful carpenter, the former philosopher who quit philosophising a long time ago, will have finished building the building. And the agonised author, pale, spectre-thin, semi-decomposed, tip-toeing at the margin of the pool recognising his or her own life while still alive in the reflection of the pool, is all at once freed of the writer's anxiety. O that thin and invisible border between the beautiful and the bizarre, the line between the beatific and the brutal. This perfect liberation from the body of this weight that lifts like a death veil, this minimalist *being* without consequence, is examined in a later artwork of the same installation artist who photocopied her naked body floating together with flying cabbages, courgettes and other vegetables resembling the figurines of Greek girls swimming up and down in time on an ancient painting from BC 450; their elastic movements caught in the moment just before they turn. One could say the artwork was organic as if alive. Human and vegetation were co-existing. Or one could say they were co-rotting, collectively decomposing. Similar to what the painter from Hertogenbosch achieves in his compendium of beasts, the Hackney artist also manages to catch the swimmer, *sans* thought, *sans* sex, *sans* worry, *sans* gender, *sans* love: *sans* because her swimmer is preoccupied purely with swimming itself. So connoisseur of correlations, naturally there is connexion between the rotting autobiographical vegetables floating around the self and the triptych's anthropomorphing beasts, bizarre, shapeshifting beings irresistibly propelling into the future on which their back is turned, while the pile of decomposing debris before them grows skyward; in the triplet we can follow history's irregular footprints from traumatic Eden to apocalyptic now. The artist, next door, with a newly composed body, part of the artwork herself, when observing the movement of shrivelling vegetables leached by water, compressed in the ecosystem of a glass tube for nine months, says she wants to catch the process of *living* and not that of dying. The split second before the body turns. Naturally, both artists display something about the bond between anatomy and art. But curious critics say the virus the artist chased all her life eventually killed her. The pathogenic bacillus the poet-physicist researched in dead bodies cost his life as well. The mysterious momentum, the second between composition and compost. Vegetation and decomposition. Viva carcass, viva giant strawberries, piss flowers, faecal poems. Viva, viva.

**[PE vii; letter VII:13]** *'...A month later, on a heartfelt, heartless day'*

...A month later, on a heartfelt, heartless day, on a cardinal day when pool reconciles body and body merges into pool, when the swimmer cleanses her body for Thanatos, not Eros, when the *pathetic* poet, pale, spectre-thin, *heart-diseased*, not quite yet absent but not present anymore, disillusioned, doomed by *desire* [i.e. 'longing for a celestial body'] and deprived of swimming pool, sick with melancholia in other words, another letter arrived: dear dying Author, we are looking for an anonymous author who will find, or perhaps invent, correlations between swimming pool and poem, hieroglyphs and horror, the pale, spectre-thin border, the hyper-real *creatura* between pre-mortem and posthumous. Aristotle in his bestiary, written circa BC350, describes the body of the swimmer in water as a one-eyed walker, a flat-bodied flâneur, clumsy, apathetic, inept being in the world. So come close, a little farther, the dying author writes in her posthumous notebook found in her Buda apartment. Look at these shortcomings on the body, the semi-designations, the splinters from exploded experiments, the ascetics of a torso: and there we saw Adam in the middle of a Budapest pool in August, happily, clumsily, ineptly impersonating a water corpse. The body of Adam, for now our fictitious drowned man is floating, his hair medusa seaweed, his pale back scorched by the midsummer Budapest sun. But dear editor, curious commissioner of meaningless missions, is this what *body* now inanimate looks like? Or is this only an intrinsic feeling, or desire, we, along with Adam, all possess? To parody our twin phantoms. With the same desire Hieronymus satirizes his own hell or Helen from Hackney, already dying, caricatures her inner dying corpse.

[*PE viii; letter VIII:13*] '...*Look, I think dead artists are*'

...Look, I think dead artists are bound to correspond with one another. The triptych of course shows us curious, pale-faced spectators, the movement of *being*, misleadingly linear, playfully chronological, between the body moving rigorously and body in rigor mortis. And so does the post-modern artist, who demonstrates the simple progress of dying by examining rotting bananas, corroding carrots, mummified mammals and fish for exactly nine months, watching, mesmerized, inquisitive, obsessed with the substance slowly turning, churning, sinking, rotting like one's own intestines, all day. But whose is this dying flesh, they both query. Body's or pool's. O water skin. Your pool is *your* tomb. Isn't there such a saying? O our inner Adam, the *tom(b)boy*, the jester, the faker, the imperfect impersonator. O the pondering parks, evaporating, in them the dead boy dancing, in them the singing, speaking fountain, before and after. No such thing as skin covering skin no matter how thick-skinned the swimmer is. No such thing as body belonging to body, the posthumous author proposes. Despite all its effort to blend in, the body, vertically, lonelily, yet non-singularly, stands out, the horizontal writer writes who occasionally looks up from his paper in the louvered window of the Great Eastern Hotel near Liverpool Street station. We too enter and take a seat next to a table opposite him. We sit and watch the posthumous author sitting and watching. He is sipping his drink away slowly, slowly staring at us through his metachromatic mind. He says he is busy right now examining parallel behavioural patterns within various micro-climates of pool and global mind, the melancholic globe. He says the key is unbelonging. To untime time. And this non-belonging, this discounting must take place artlessly, intuitively, telepathically. This we might call happiness. As happy as a mausoleum can be.

## [PE ix; letter IX:13] '...Dear floating flâneur'

...Dear floating flâneur, on the last day of the season, on a thinking, feeling day when pool reconciles body and body forgives pool when it is snowing outside and inside and the pool is closed and open too like a script with open ending, we decided to find Merleau-Ponty's crypt. And on that thinking, feeling, snowy day, when anything could be covered and uncovered, we found and paused at the tomb that, in a random, deserted site, semi-lit by dim neon light illuminated for the sightseer who, now standing close, had travelled from afar. And we too, stood there, somewhat illuminated, half levitating above the tomb at dusk when all things look like something else, for at dusk nothing is but what is not. The philosopher's tomb, we could say, called us to come close to keep a distance. And we went close enough and kept a distance and when we were close and distant enough we saw that certain dates flickering on the tombs were unstoppably rolling towards exactly where we stood. The annual doomsday doomed to catch up with the day it was doomed to ruin. Behind us. Now ahead of us. And so as we stood there among other mourners mourning ourselves we saw an autumn burial in a fin-de-siècle grandiose Budapest pantheon. This pantheon was pompous like a sculpture park with exotic plants and poets' sculpted figures gathered in the park all in some kind of irrational pause; Rilke, for instance with giant angel wings, Rimbaud, bathing in semi-lit halo, nagging the Witch to speak. Celan's fragile figure set in lotus pose at the margin of his empty grave composing an alternative [*todes*]fugue with an alternative ending, Keats, pale, spectre-thin, wearing an apothecary's gown, next to him Shelley always already drowned, W. S. Graham in a jovial walking pose presumably still walking on the wordroad

home, Attila József's posture slightly twisted,
cervical spine fractured and with only one arm,
Catullus, portrait of the lover, the loather, tormented,
*crucified* by loathing and loving. And there, right
above the poet torsos was a giant arc, a terrific and
terrifying rainbow. And as we were standing there at
the edge of Merleau-Ponty's pool, his miniature
basin, the tiny patio, the rectangularity, the depth,
the width, and height, the dampness, drew the
obvious analogy. Dear thanatomaniac, dear grave
robber, there and then, the sight of the crypt, the
white page, the walk in the pompous pantheon
among other white-washed tombs, the minute long
pause at the margin of the tiny tetragon, on the
marble the hazy hieroglyphs, the act of reading
itself, the deciphering of dead data, names written in
water, brought with it peace too, equilibrium. And I
thought of sickness. Mother's choleric old sheepdog.
Her melancholic organs. The lungs full of fluids.
Her failing, feeling heart deformed from pain. And I
then thought of aphorisms too, quietly humming, not
mentioning it to my nameless acquaintance allergic
to what he calls poor aporias. And I thought of the
triptych, the different swimming shapes and
techniques, how in-pool-body metamorphoses into
another, an amphibian, a vertebra, a fluid butterfly, a
tadpole even, a centaur, a lover, and I thought of the
bad swimmer who, despite all the swimming
lessons, still swims like a mosquito, legs hanging
downwards, as if longing to drown, who, on his
chance day will forget that all along and on all
occasions it was to do with resisting resistance. And
I thought of my own phantom swimmer, the
posthumous poet's desire to learn the vocabulary of
desire while we are alive. That in that moment
standing at the edge of the pool, I saw the pool, *my*
pool, the right pool, next to the old hospital run by
Brothers Hospitallers. It was another thinking,
feeling day, a mundane day, an *undaring*. On the
surface of the water the body of the former swimmer

was wandering, drifting, floating, gradually blending in to the autumn canopy of the pool, the bronze body fading into auburn leaves fallen from nearby chestnut trees. And in that moment I was alpha and omega, subject and object, patient and potion, I was page, I was editor, I was illness and medication. I was the world I was composing and I was the I that was being composed, I was part and whole but I was *pars pro toto*. And I knew that I, as *part*, was *wholly* part of this world. I was synaesthesia. And so, I thought, a good poem should be.

[PE x; letter X:13] '...Dear non-swimmer'

...Dear non-swimmer. The truth is that I never regretted spending my entire life in the swimming pool. And so dear Doubter, other than totally empty, isn't it easier to imagine the pool, the triptych, our universe, inhabited by magic and mirage, milliard types of fishes and figures, finned and finless, swimming seraphim and acrobatic archangels? For darkness is only darkness when illuminated. Remember Adam who the other day in a Budapest spa threw his body on the surface of the water impersonating a water corpse? The trick, Adam then said between two breaths, is not to give away that you are only joking. To fake the techniques of the drowned man. To learn the learnings of the lifeless by heart. To re-construct the architecture of the floating body with your own, limbs relaxed, lightheaded, the lifeless swimmer mimicking the lazy one. There is a recent retro photo of Karine Laval's pool series online that Adam, who survived the mimicking exercise, sent me one winter. In one of the many photos the swimmer's body looks as if one leg were amputated. The other limb, the only limb, disproportionately long and thin, almost flimsy, propelled the body artlessly as if she could slip through your hands. The same limbless swimmer I saw years ago in Norwich's Olympic Pool. Her horizontal torso was gliding through water, the fastest in the pool. And all at once it all made sense. Since non-sense is only non-sense till it becomes the norm, i.e. common sense. Resisting resistance means *limblessness*. It means dissolution, suspension. Where your body ends the pool begins. There is one and only body and this one and only body does not *belong*. Or more precisely it *un*belongs to pool. And naturally, we all recognise that the swimmer's *one* and *only* body was the original, the archetypal swimmer inside the swimmer inside we long to find. But critically we never really review the absolute poem inside the poem inside. The ideal poem all editors doubt. But if there were an absolute poem, a poem as large as the world, the posthumous poet writes in her notebook found in her Buda apartment, in this poem there would be two images photographed together, which become visible on the picture with two contours, two heads, two different connotations. Two swimming bodies, one of the dead and one of the live, more or less overlapping each other, moving gradually away from their own outlines, drifting away, emerging. In this paradigm poem, which naturally does not exist, each swimmer would relinquish something of its own identity, emerging into the other temporarily, or for longer, and would bring about a third entity; the hybrid swimmer. A motionless swimmer who carries the motioning swimmer inside and outside. But dear Doubter, isn't it this doubted 'oneness' [*Notebook*, 123], this speculative identity, this somewhat fusible and permeated soul who the swimmer was while she was swimming alive in the pool, the world, which was wholly inside and where she was wholly outside herself? Wasn't she, the swimmer, the poem, resisting resistance, denying all along, on all occasions, her swimmer body longing to intermingle with other swimming bodies, bodies that belonged to her, bodies that belonged to others, the dissection of the world's phenomena into separate objects? O swimmer, wash your body for Thanatos, not Eros. The same routine: clip toe nails, shave lower legs, wax bikini lines, later, all androgenic hair. In other words: swim speedier. Love faster. O posthumous poet, prepare the body, once pre-mortem, for the public eye. O the loathing loving water globe, o Laocoon world. In which everyone is someone else. O the phantom swimmer who is enfolding us, holding us too tight. The drowned pen that pins us down. Verticality. Eureka. Eureka. The password of the swimmer to another world is simulation.

[PE xi; letter XI:13] '... *Apo phainesthai ta phainomena*'

...Apo phainesthai ta phainomena. Let what shows itself be seen from itself, just as it shows itself from itself. Do you remember the stuffed whale in *The Melancholy of Resistance*? It was raining in the town for nine years non-stop when the whale arrived overnight, eerie messenger, with a dodgy Russian travelling circus. In the novel the gigantic mammal's body stuffed, preserved, mummified, was displayed in the middle of the marketplace of the town unmarked on any maps floating somewhere in Central-Eastern Europe. Naturally, there was no way for this whale to blend into our reality because the body, despite it being there with large wide open eyes, was gone. The whale was deceased. His body, at the town's focal point: *inappropriate.* In the novel the stuffed body is persistently the target of anger and adoration while it lies there silent, stiff, stoic. And although its peeling corpse smells horrendous, the enormous cadaver looks beautiful and bizarre. And although it is wordless, it speaks to us of flower and flesh. It speaks of glorious plummets, dignity and, naturally, of the vast ocean. It speaks of what drowning really means: the parody of all whales, the paradox of fishing mammals out of the sea. That whale composed in the novel, there, in the middle of the nameless muddy town, dreams of being decomposed as opposed to the swimmer who longs to be preserved. Look, dear dreamer of the absolute composition. Adam sent me another short film of Laval the other day, on a winter's day, the drowning day, the daring, with a female swimmer gliding through the pool water. In the motioning of the slow moving film it feels as if the swimmer were in fact static and as if it were only the movement of the water creating the illusion of any motion. The film gives its trick away when the swimmer's head suddenly moves towards the surface and eventually surfaces. But it is in the split second exposure again, in between the surfacing and surfacing when the swimmer's face expands into a monster's, metamorphoses into a cry or a distorted roar or a scream.

[*PE xii; letter XII:13*] '... *Last Sunday you sent me*'

...Last Sunday you sent me a segment of your essay you were in the middle of writing. In the passage you explain that in a letter to his friend John Reynolds of the 3$^{rd}$ of May 1818, the poet-physicist, our composer of fear, fearer of decomposition, *pre mortem*, writes that he hopes that *post mortem*, like the gull, or a good-sized fish, he may dip crosswise across the page, and, *post scriptum*, he will not vanish out of sight – (Letters 1: 280). O private alphas and public omegas. O Lethe. Personally, posthumously, from where I stand, instead of falling across the page, I'll prefer to make my way towards the margin. O the pondering childhood parks, evaporating, in them the private dancing, the speaking fountains. In them the small amphora body which we loved and loathed while we were alive, now, look, a solid *metaphora*. But dear decipherer of composition. *This* book is now semi-lit, semi-closed. From where I stand the conclusion won't make any difference. The debate, as to which direction the body falls finally, from where you stand will always be indifferent. O apathetic lover *sans* soul, *sans* silhouette, *sans* passion. The swimming pool is semi-lit, semi-light. *Odi et amo* [*quare id faciam?*]. Salute and farewell. And so, look, stoic other, the posthumous poet continues in her notebook found in her Buda apartment, today's swimming day is the last day, the appearing day, the becoming day, the composing, to do it *sensibly* on the page. To navigate the body home through language with compassion as if our (eternal) life were not ours but belonged to someone else. The expiring day, the disappearing, when swimming pool forgives swimmer and swimmer adapts to pool. You might call it the swimmer's transubstantiation. The swimmer who exits the pool is the same swimmer who entered pre mortem, even if, post-swimming, no outward changes are apparent to the eye. The body look, unchanged, unaltered, wears the same pre-swimming face. And yet the manner in which the change occurs is a mystery. When we use the word *change*, we by no means think it explains the mode by which the body of the swimmer is converted into the ideal body of the post-swimming swimmer the swimmer has been searching for all her life, for this is altogether incomprehensible. But we mean this change not figuratively, metaphorically or symbolically, nor by any extraordinary grace attached to it and yet we mean that the body during its regular and everyday swim, becomes verily and indeed essentially the very true and same body it appeared before it disappeared. And so in the half-lit, half-illuminated neon-light we enter the local pool and we undress quietly. And leaving the body behind us we dive into the pool, the familiar pool, the same pool, the only pool. Nothing much has changed since we were gone. Objects are in their right place, in their right time; simple, safe paraphernalia. On the surface of the water, look, the book bores Dodo still floating artlessly on its back. Small fish clipped of wings vanishes underwater. Girlboy diseased from strawberry in dark corner. At the edge of the pool lion in neon light (with small black reptile caught in its jaws), elephant and giraffe stare *away*. Porcupine, somewhat panicking, rushes off the page.

[**PE xiii; letter XIII:13**] *'Viva la pool'*

Viva la pool *sans* silhouette, *sans* swimmer. Viva empty pool.

[ ‡ *Postscript, Miscellanea; I:1*] *'Torch bearer, faithful concierge'*

Torch bearer, faithful concierge; bear the torch for me for a little longer and guide me through the labyrinth to the last pool. Look, it happened to me on an August day when light is darker and the shadows longer, on an anniversary day when the nation celebrates itself being a nation, on a day which unends with trumpets, fireworks and trombones, that all of a sudden such melancholia came over me that I lost the will to give my usual daily visit to the pool. I spent two hours contemplating in my steam bath staring at the four tiled walls gathering courage to be able to do anything productive at all. Finally after hours of inertia and pathos (o *bathos*), I recomposed myself and strolled down the Buda hills not far enough to reach the Olympic pool that's next to Lukács Spa along the Danube, but close enough to arrive at the local pool perched on the slopes of the Buda hills which advertises itself quietly with the outer sign, as if scribbled by a child, stuck just above the small entrance, on my way unnoticing the silence and irregular lethargy of the streets. The clouds hung low and light rain sprinkled the cobbled network of the XI district. Entering the pool I passed by the attendant at the pay desk and made my way through the narrow corridors semi-lit, semi-light. I undressed quietly in the changing room and entering the small swimming arena I saw that the pool was empty. Not a single soul in either of the lanes, the pool stood there still *sans* swimmers, *sans* silhouettes, *sans* instructor, the elderly caretaker with a jingling keyring normally taking care of the pool's entrance and exit was missing too, the pool stood there *sans* its banterers who would sit on the yellow plastic chairs bantering away their usual summer banters, *sans* life guard in white t-shirt in the corner cabin guarding the lives of his swimmers while their bodies swim up and down, *sans* wet towels, *sans* empty dressing gowns of fellow swimmers regularly left behind to suggest that there at least had been someone there before I arrived but had exited by the time I entered. Other than the tiny blue rescue net leaning against the white wall, big enough only to rescue a small child, or a larger fish, all swimming apparatus was out of sight. Senselessly, I started my usual lengths with a sublime thrill and otherworldly greed you feel when you can have the whole pool to yourself. The empty pool, the swimmer knows, is a rare and hybrid moment of chance and mercy. The perfectly still sheet of water was only disturbed by my own front crawl cutting into the water, body inching to and fro between the two tiled ends. They say pools are uneventful places but there and then I secretly hoped for and anticipated *the* event. But the swimming pool stood still, *sans* silhouettes, *sans* souls, *sans* swimmers either in the water or on the margins, *sans* life guard in white t-shirt watching me swimming up and down so I feared, if I were to get a stroke or a heart attack, no one would come to my rescue, that I would helplessly, lonelily drown. Yet I continued the front crawl to and fro and to and fro between the two ends of the pool, faster and faster, each stroke each time stronger and weightier, speed increasing, heartbeat swifter, until I felt that by each crawl I too got more outraged, with each strike into water more caustic, more competitive, more choleric. And through this fury and frustration which I couldn't explain to myself, I peered out of my goggles: the swimming pool stood still *sans* silhouette, *sans* swimmers, *sans* souls of banterers on the yellow plastic chairs bantering away their usual summer pool banters. My goggles got wet inside but I knew they did not leak because my expensive Speedo goggles would never let me down so I knew the water was leaking inside the goggles, in other words, inside the swimmer inside. And by each stroke my body got more vengeful to and froing, to and froing between the two tiled ends, each length speedier, faster, weightier until the moment when speed could not get speedier, in other words until speed could not exceed its own speed, after which all this fury was reversed and weight got lighter, swim flimsier, and I did not know in which pool I was swimming or more precisely it felt as if I had been swimming in an otherworldly pool or more precisely as if I had been swimming in the pool of another body's world. At which point I did not know whether my body was stiff or swimming, if I was motionless or motioning an inch closer towards either end, uncertain if I were a swimmer *sans* silhouette, *sans* soul, or if I was no longer a swimmer swimming in the pool but merely a particle of pool, whether I was wholly part of the whole or if I was *pars pro toto*; whether I, the former swimmer, now *sans* silhouette, *sans* soul, were a composite of the swimming pool that stood there *sans* swimmers, *sans* silhouette, *sans* souls. And then, after a long levitating hour, or so it seemed, in the milieu of the swimming pool *sans* silhouettes, *sans* swimmers, *sans* soul, as I was to and froing between the two blue tiled margins, I saw a body of a swimmer sinking slowly, slowly towards the bottom of the pool. When she reached the bottom tiles her one foot kicked her body off again upwards towards the neon light and her figure metamorphosed into a perfect butterfly. A moment later, when another swimmer joined the pool and later on many others until the pool was as full as a pool should be, I understood that making sense of the senseless does not make any sense, that there is no such thing as infernal pool or celestial pool, that pools don't fade and pools don't hide, pools don't meta-morph or anthropo-morph, that this pool is the only pool, the same pool, the right pool and there are no swimming pools in Canaan. And so, to get more clarity, for more enlightenment I pulled my goggles off and soon recognised the figures of two elderly banterers bantering away on the plastic yellow chairs; I spotted the perfect life guard, who, during my timeless, misplaced hour, had mastered the perfect tan, watching us from his miniature cabin, guarding the lives of his daily swimmers swimming up and down, and I saw the eager instructor explaining to small children from one of the blue tiled ends how to swim sensibly as if your (eternal) life were at stake, and the elderly caretaker with a jingling keyring, who also, by then, took care of both water and dry land. After finishing my usual lengths, I rested my upper body with both elbows on one of the tiled ends, lost, watching from inside the late summer rain outside stroking the glass. The rage, that had captured me earlier, with all choleric strokes and lengthless lengths, had swum out of my body like a competitive swimmer, who already had reached the other side, but this other, lazier body I was resting with on my elbows at this end of the pool, felt all at once at rest. I took my cap off too and through the glass that separated inside from outside, I recognised the quiet outer sign for the building gesturing towards the outside, inviting the silent street inside for a brief swim. The sign read: *LOOP GNIMMIWS.*

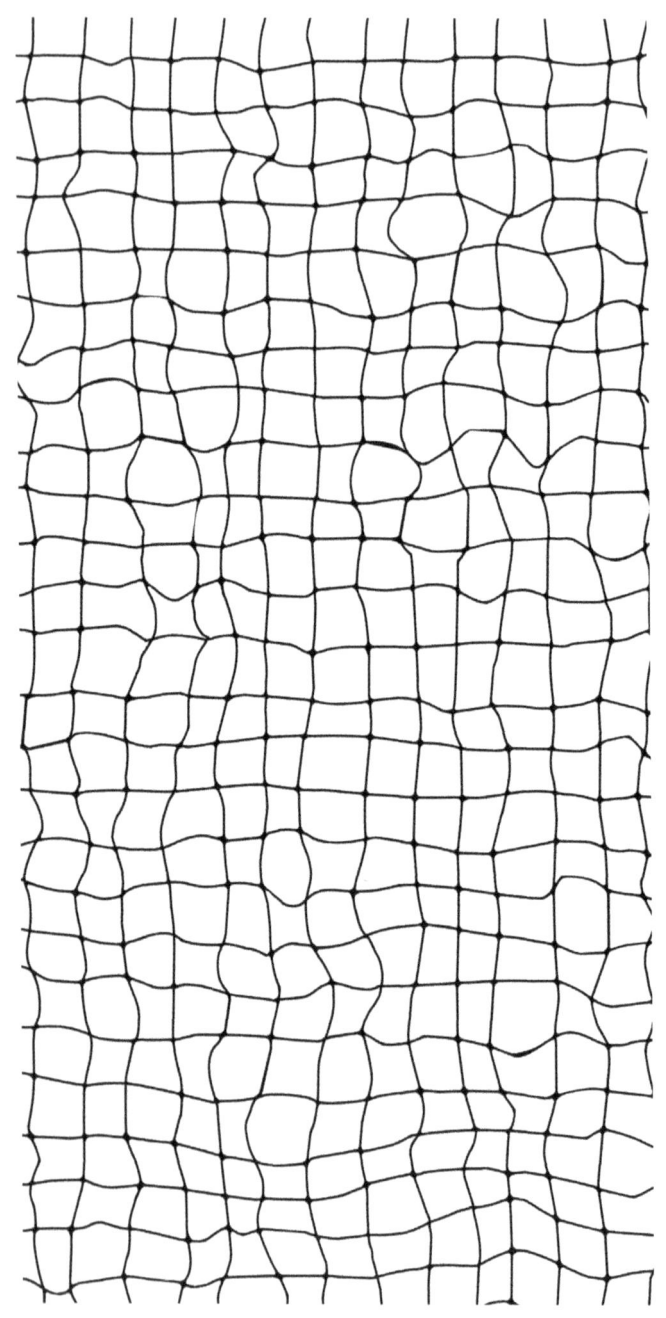

*Book Three*

**Fall of Pool**

[Postcard 3]

I am in Basel, land-locked but a man-made meeting point of languages and countries. Confused at the airport I entered the wrong one, but water finds its way through, like conversation. There is a practice here in Basel of putting your clothes in a swim bag and floating down the river on the current. I will do it for you, though scared, swimmer. Water is always a test, like conversation, it knows no borders (though in a wealthy part of Athens there are closet pools, secret pools, hidden under AstroTurf and boards, avoiding pool tax, hiding from the sky).

Thoughts here are drenched with Shakespeare's watery words; King Richard wants his friends' tears to spell 'sorrow' on the earth, Ophelia has had too much of water, she does not need her brother's tears, or even a long speech about a gem set in a silver sea, a jewel island, a natural fortress: how to say those words *tonight*?

Our audiences are hot in a room without air conditioning. The live stream carries the work on, down river to screens in rooms, to hand-held devices, to you? Tomorrow, though landlocked, I will swim for you, with my clothes in a bag, though the image, now, reaches Basel soaked in other associations. Tomorrow the current could carry me from one country to another.

We do not swim alone.

Terry O'Connor, 'The second of September, a card from Switzerland'

*Part One*

**Letters from Lacrima**

[*The Swimmers' Discourse*]

[....and so the writer of water, waterlover, watercarrier, mapmaker of swimming pools, the fluent etymologist who reconstructs the no-word from abundance, from lack, the anonymous water typist, pale, spectre-faced, seriously dehydrated, staring at the outside from a fluid inside, an aquatic interior at the physical, the dreaded exterior, from the top floor office cubicle, one's inner balistraria (for isn't being in the world being in resistance), gazing inwardly outward at the manic (minute by minute) erection of The Diamond – which at some point was also named the Jewel in the Crown – idea soon dropped – a post-mortem of the Edwardian Jessop Hospital for women, an £81 million state-of-the-art construction, fifty shades of grey soon to be lit up and the door opened to growth and investment, making a colossal contribution to regional economy and the new engineering generation of the globe, locked up in a body immovable, unbelonging, walled up in the static, the entropic, the concrete, daydreaming of another body, belonging, being/moving fluidly in the pool within a familiar, also always typed, water discourse with the lover, the swimmer, a discourse always already about and of water, longing to be elsewhere, decided to type her first response to her silent correspondent, an embryonic attempt to become a *collaborateur* of a, you could reason, long overdue summer tête-à-tête heart to heart, with the posthumous poet, the horizontal author, the silent swimmer, who, pre-mortem cooperates willingly with her reader, also always dying, yet still alive, from and to the other side, desirably, post scriptum, in two, three, or many alphabets in an attempt to dialogue, inter alia, about private catastrophes or universal loves whose choreography or cartography we don't yet know. And so the letter begins: 'Each summer was a mystery. Each pool a chance. A secret...']

[**Pool letter 1.1 typed, Misc. i**]

Under maintenance.

[*On Catastrophe*]

Each summer was a mystery. Each pool a chance.
Each poem a secret. But after unbuilding comes the
building, a reversal of what is expected to take place.
O aquatic typewriter that types lines between the lines.
Keep love alive while the typing lasts. At a time when
the poem (knowledge and perception) like an artificial
pond, unattended, algae-dense, is murky, *sans* mercy,
*sans* transparency, in what way, one wonders, should
one proceed then towards the poem's seabed, the final
resting place of these conflicting conversations, the
poem, our Ithaca, the poem, our swimming pool, the
poem, our shared fluid tomb whose geography, or
borders, we don't yet know or see, I mean a writing
that calls for thinking, the one that tickles souls. How
can the anonymous swimmers, the posthumous lovers
recognise shapeless, muffled symbols underwater? Is
one's own inner global disaster, one's private history,
auto-nautical crises, lighter, flimsier, even faster,
when occurring, and/or experienced, as a swimming
pool event? And if so with what methods does the
water typist underwater type absurdities, ambiguities,
unnameables, micro and macro climaxes of this
summer vis-à-vis, heart to heart, between two
irreconcilable cartographed others, and disentangle
entangled cyclops, and other species of figures of
speech in aqua, in the liquefied poem (what is the
ultimate point), how will we make sense of the
amorous swimmers' incomprehensible, incompatible
discourse? For them each summer offered a mystery.
Each pool a chance. Each poem a secret. Each chance
a call for comprehension, for a thinking feeling
thought en route (again) to Sebald's East Anglian
melancholic seashore which now, in our poor aporia,
will be our assembly point, where we finally gather
ourselves together, in an ideal marginality, at the edge
of this island, in the absolute horizontality where one

needs to apologize to the other retro-futuristically in a one way correspondence for anything one once will or would have said (before), for all the tricks and all the foul play, all the cheating, all the double-meaning, always somehow ahead of oneself in the past. The calligrapher thinks (might you call it being *under duress*) the closest perhaps we could ever get to the other's catastrophe, the fictitious, cataclysmic event, would be to picture the writer, the other, the amorous lover on his final (death)drive (if you will) in Norfolk (towards your seashore), camera attached to his smart forehead when his car crashes with a lorry in Poringland on the Lowestoft Road in the midst of his East Anglian mindscape. And then imagine, you, the alternative other, were you to watch it back on youtube and immediately, as experience a priori yet right after the event, you'd report it back to the world. After building comes the unbuilding. So what shall we talk about in our last summer discourse? And when and where shall we meet our own event, at what detour, at what passage? It'll soon turn into a game of one player chess, you'll see, the game of lonely typing; thinking against time. And although the klaviatur now almost animate & intimate (if you will), script made (un)familiar or even uncann*y* like the strange familiarity of swimming in a swimming pool, immersive perhaps in order to impress the silent literatist, the wordless lettrist, the deaf typist, the posthumous co-author, (the dead reader – if you will), our inner paralytic, numb armchair psychotherapist, perhaps we could proceed on the meridian instead eventually always returning to where we started – with nothing said, felt, thought, not to have moved an inch – collectively, dialogically or otherwise. Or should *we* today (if you will) perhaps move with the movement of a perplexed swimmer, or some kind of paraphyletic mammal in water, as if swimming to and fro in our story, our local swimming pool, face turned backwards towards the past yet body propelled unstoppably into the future, shifting – thinking, swimming, remembering, even – inch by inch ahead of ourselves in time, a centaur, or an amphibian, a one-eyed aquatic flâneur, half-here, semi-there, flight tipped somewhat sideways in horizontal, historic, histrionic here-&-nows? It's not the vision but the motion, Aristotle writes. Not comedy, but tragedy that renders absolute completion to the play. Without our inner catastrophic lover, *we* are lost for ever.

[Pool letter 1.2 typed, Misc. ii]

No swimming beyond this point.

[**Pool letter 1.3 typed, Misc. iii**]

No diving no diving no diving no

[*On Fear*]

Dear typewriter. Happiness of, within or around the poem is not impossible or unachievable because language's (our inner typewriter's) automatic drive to permeate in some kind of hydrostatic, pre or post semiotic (*sans* sentence, *sans* meaning) abundance or chance, or let alone because of its ultimate desire to become inanimate, that is, to go silent, to say nothing, or simply to cease to be, but because of its condition, its melancholy, the poem's global guilt to be licensed, offered the canonical (political) chance of being extraordinary or just simply exceptional, in other words legible, comprehensible (a comprehension also always followed by collective purring and humming) or just simply directly, or didactically directed to, i.e. literally deciphered, that is understood. Dear typewriter (dear heart) that which types lines between the lines on water for the dehydrated reader who can read lines between the lines, it is, they say, the swimmer's historic moment to stay calm. Look, dying reader, deficit of water, the figure of the amoraphobic lover to or about whom the typewriter types always already metamorphoses into another loathing lover during the course of writing the book of oblivious swimmers who swim and love through life (for now, our page) *sans* sense, *sans cor*, *sans* passion. And it is because the writing is not taking place on but around the margin of the page (for now the edge of our pool), in air and water within the swimmer's rhythmic breathing, pressure and oxygen supplied by aqualungs (in other words the free flow of air from the cylinder to the breathing organ), within our arrhythmic correlations between air and water, body and pool, body and lover, in the irreconciliations of which our most irregular or random associations blur into the one and only correlation, our absolute intimate relation. So then how can I or you be happy when I am or you are not, you may rightly ask. But there is another place within all locations. A public pronouncement, a definitive yes within negations, a *dénouement* that may settle your doubts. Another concrete swimming pool within the fluid pool. A resistance in all surfaces which yet offers a simple, irresistible reading of the writing. Take, for instance, this spot from where I am writing the writing to you. From the centre of the pool, the focal point of absolute solitude, the hermetic heart of the poem and yet with the openness of the heart. Take the philosophy of the awful binary, for our example. A terrific synchronism, an inventive cohabitation; and so imagine a holiday as homicide. Atrocity camouflaged as (tourist) attraction. How will it all end, you may also wonder. Will it be drowning, fading, or the simple quiet/unseen failure of the heart in the middle of swimming a pool length? In the middle of these automatic exercises we know very little of the body, say the swimmer's nervous system, the typist's metabolism, or the lover's coronary circulation, let alone of the *cor* itself (the main organ which supplies the movement of the swimmer, the typing of the typist, the loving of the lover with blood, with love) embellished in décor. Your own deep structure. The anatomy of the poem. Climax and anti-climax co-exist, real and hyper-real coincide, collide; they don't come in chronological order; all sorts of catastrophic events, unimaginable, could be taking place inside without awareness of outside. Take for another example (try and imagine) the East German lido *Friedrichroda pool* on a 1930s postcard sent to you from Thüringia. The swimming pool within a deeper, darker swimming pool reflects the movement of the swimmer within a much deeper movement of a darker swimmer, or a much darker movement of a deeper swimmer, the phantom I within the deeper, darker I. You may call this the psychosis of the pool. The archetype of all simulacra. And yet the sleepy swimmer, inattentive to peril, oblivious to danger, *sans* sense, *sans* thought, *sans* sense of place or time, as if swimming in some embryonic eden or hydraulic apathy, confides in simulation. And so the posthumous poet's post-anticipation, this kind of post-traumatic creative thrill, the post-remembering artist's gratification, is always spectrally surrounded by disappointment, displeasure and pain. Architecture (*your* architecture, the poem's Aristotelian structure), an idyllic postcard, in which, you or I, camouflaged, say, as the pool's quiet concierge, or as the cabin attendant or disguised as the pool's life guard, or perhaps the harmless historian, the diligent typist, ready (inside and outside) to commit the dreaded *historic* deed, and with one single word, movement, sign, whistle or other hissing sound we conduct the global erasure of all silent swimmers who swim oblivious to the approaching peril in the pool, busy practising the right breathing exercise, preoccupied with resisting resistance. Later, when we look at the postcard (the East German artist sent me) with swimmers in the lido peacefully swimming up and down in history, our local swimming pool, with (our) ghosts long gone from the tall diving /watch towers, we tremble without knowing why. This you may call the absolute dread. The infinite mysterium. The absolute apprehension when the mottephobic I apprehends you because I don't comprehend you, o poem, o moth. I can't seize or grasp you without dread. In fact I anticipate you with dread, i.e. I both tremble and I am fascinated. *I* fears you, is what I fear with the knowing lack of knowing where your body ends and where it continues in the movement of the chronological flow of unstoppable events. It's the lack of seizure of authority, the psychoanalyst says. And authorship, you may add. But why do we dread the other, the swimming lover who lacks borders, outline, fixity, or fear. Fearless, loveless swimmer, although *water corpses* as real phenomena do not exist in your lexis, Hévíz, *locus vulgarites Hewyz dictus*, the largest natural spa on the Central European lido map, is renowned as the place that naturally collects *them*. At the edge of the eco-lido there is a fin-de-siècle sanatorium where I saw the algae mother, the former gymnast, last winter (and naturally I still keep seeing her) who complained about rheumatic problems in the knees and joints. This kind of trembling of metamorphosed lidos is the arthritic mother's tremble too. Or yours, for that reason. We tremble at the sight of the non-sight (I for that reason, tremble at anyone and anything these days). At the real sight behind the superficial site. At the superficial sight disguising the real template. The commercial postcard that sells a slaughterhouse as wildlife or rest resort. So this mother, from the winter spa, talks of her fear of drowning in the lake, conjuring visions of her frail body pulled down by corals and water lilies to the bottom where lots of past patients had found their resting place. The lake is just too deep despite its temperature being very warm even in the winter because of the natural spa's unpredictable force caused by the suction of undercurrents. The mother says she was worried that her feeble, rheumatic body or her arthritic legs would get entangled in the underwater vegetation and that the guard whose job is to guard the swimmers from his watch tower at that random moment of history would forget to look. They say there are many undiscovered, lost water corpses, including the skeletons of the rescue divers who also had disappeared, lying at the bottom of the sanatorium's lake and she shows me newspaper cuttings to prove her fear is justified. In other words she was worried that she would become a water corpse; a fear that was real for her because she did not know if she was partly part of the lido or wholly part of the lido, if she was completely apart from the world or if she was pars pro toto. And so, I thought, a good poem should be. Dear callous calligrapher. Our unfeeling, unthinking inner typist. Today, standing at the edge of the pool we saw very little of the world. It's because today the poem we saw eclipsed the poem we write and the poem we searched for was unconcealed. Pars pro toto. The poem was wholly outside and yet it was wholly inside itself. Overshadowing the real it was taken from. Look, to overcome fear we must understand affection (affection to animate while we were alive, attraction to become inanimate while we are alive), the water painter, painter of swimming pools claims in his final fragment, o curious poet, what's another word, a better word, *the just word* for *swimming pool*. What's a more substantial word for mask, conceit, disguise? But there is another language within language than noise. An *absolute writing* that attempts, not so much to surpass the limit of itself but create utterance beyond sound or any sense. The muffled discourse of the swimmers, the roar of the hysterical historian, the whimper of the lovers, or even the silence of cyclops and centaurs. This approximation to the truth is a leaning toward stillness. The tongue of the darkest unnameables, direst dread and deepest desire. This, perhaps, *nothing* to say fills us with mystery. The closest I could get to the spectre is by imagining a busy outdoor spa in winter with the water corpse of my frail algae mother half floating, half drowning in the sanatorium's outdoor spa; her body entangled with water lilies and exotic underwater plants. It also fills us with inexplicable melancholy, stoic unfeeling, phlegmatic frustration with which we let go of the conversation. Not because the text will be lonely or may remain unread but because letting it go means letting go of the body we loved while we were alive. As if you were descending or diving without aqualungs well under 25 or even 70 meters deep. The decadent bar on the surface of every square centimetre of the skin and 250.000 Pascal on the mind, on the poem, on the body of the typewriter, the heavy type machine, the heart, is heavier than air and it leaves us unfeeling, unthinking, weighty and emptiful. Woolf, the wingless lover, the notorious algae mother is a corporeal proof, by now a trope, a symbol, that *water corpse* is a phenomenon of all languages we speak or nonetheless comprehend.

It's Saturday late August afternoon, the posthumous author writes a few seconds before she drowns (in retrospective linear order), and I am at Komjádi pool again, perhaps for the last time this summer. Water temperature is the usual 26 degrees. The lido-scape seems blissful. And yet, scarcely perceptible, there is an eerie winterish breath in the Budapest air which makes the surface of the swimming pool unsettled, nervous, psychedelic. And the position of the body in its finale needs to be ideal, beautiful, idyllic. Look, swimmer, homecomer in disguise, our shifty-eyed Odysseus is now's horrid hero, a devious long-distance lover, who is making for home, by the wrong way, on the wrong courses. Let the poem tremble, let it be a secret, let it overcome fear of happiness. Let it be our *contradictio in adiecto*, mystory's circuitous path from you to you. Algae mother. Hyper-real lover. Callous calligrapher. Let the poem, the body, the other get entangled, lost, dragged down into deep dark.

[Pool letter 1.4 typed, Misc. iv]

no lifeguard on duty no lifeguard on duty no lifeguard

[Pool letter 1.5 typed, Misc. v]


swim at your own risk swim at your own risk swim

[*Chronicles of Shame*]

"*our doors are as wide open as our hearts*"
(Sanatorium of Brothers Hospitallers and Kaiser's Bath, Buda, 1806)

And so unbelonging to timelessness or time, imagine our swimmer, on a leaping day, a misplaced day, on a day familiarised as *other*, absent, defamiliarised as accident or supplement, a surplus in pool's global diary adapted to keep the solar system synchronised, in which the year too was wandering as *no* event, apocryphal insignificance, *sans* any historic turbulence in some kind of meteorological miasma, atemporally adrift in a temporary chronological amnesia or coincidence, imagine our supplement swimmer, the supplementary figure *I* supplementing I drifting in a pool populated by other drifting extras, part but wholly part of pool, a pool apart but wholly part of a global fog and this international fog part of a much foggier, forgotten era, and so imagine this pioneer *I*, a mutable Budapest *iota* on the nautical map muting in mutability from *Alpha* to *Beta*, swimming in a pool paralleling pool, being in a world in which the world was world, not disparate but total, not analogy but tautology, in Margaret Island's repetitive fluid magna flora, its substance substantial, its measure measured in chance and mercy, with the budding body of the young swimmer's euphoria and jubilation. And so my dear scribe inside the anti-scribe, let us imagine a winter in this drifting almanac, drifting inside and outside, an outside which was still connected to the inside, a type of connection fog helps us comprehend, by a narrow underwater tunnel leading the liminal swimmer, still not quite lost, still not quite yet found, liminally drifting to and fro in a hydraulic passage from the tiled inside to the tiled outside, and for this nascent, phantom I derived from fog, and the fog from an era in disguise, who was both inside and outside *our* story, that was both outside and inside a

much grander story, for this emerging swimmer, a
superfluous, swimming diorama among other swimming
data, submerged in language's unstoppable flow, who
does not quite know yet how to swim, think, write or
loathe or love, restless, like figurines in one's first *ábécé*
or *alphabeta* (floating from *Alpha* to *Beta*, *Omega*, to
*Lethe*), the primary within the posthumous poet, the
latter, still dormant, still silent, still still in the body of
the former, everything was what it was even though I
could not figure out accurately what was what; yet the
cosmological conviction that the pool was pool, the
swimming lanes visual signs to help the juvenile to
process the pool in small pools, in smaller portions of
the much larger pool, a micro pool within a macro pool
belonging to the swimmer's body and body belonging to
fog, fog to pool, the world, and I, the minute, premature
swimmer, a small centaur, part of swimming pool, part
of fog, was tangible, even if the world in fog for the
advanced swimmer sounds or seems intangible, in other
words, unimaginable, undefinable, unnameable with any
other name other than itself. At early dawn, the close of
day this kind of euphoria with which the pool's fog
embraced me was oddly familiar, like a stranger's
embrace. And in this unfamiliar enfolding of fog the
pool was pool, the life guard guarded lives, the cleaner
cleaned blue tiles of the tiled inside and tiled outside,
and above and below, our life guard who guarded our
lives was a concrete *Epsilon* etcetera, except the bronze
bodied Olympic swimmer, the thermodynamic human
Alpha or Delta, half deity, half aqua, who fills the
common swimmer with awe and pride. So viva
hydraulic hyper real swimmer. Viva simulacra. But
look, *aw*ful, fearful swimmer, when we swim from pool
to pool, Omega to Gamma, margin to margin, we swim
from past to past, in a pool half full, half emptiful, and
so our now-pool is perpetually eclipsed, overcast, veiled
by hazy history, wholly part of *ourstory*, and so our
instant view, our immediate panorama in this pool, like
miasma, is always already obscured, a single story
which we post-a posteriori hope to experience as

antiquity, as *epos*, in other words, a superhuman event, or a series of herculean incidents or coincidences a priori, Esterházy, the posthumous author, set in lotus position at the margin of our pool post fog era, writes in *Harmonia Caelestis*, whose harmonious death made the skies open above the city and from this disharmonious sky, as from the wound of the dead lover, the wounded poem or the unarmoured author, by now unarmed, stretched out, harmlessly, horizontally on a renaissance medical atlas, body incised, cut open, in order to understand, not only the new, estranged human but the new, estranged human texture, its *humani corporis fabrica* (given that there is autopsy, given that the autopsy is requested by loved ones, given that there is love, etcetera), the century's filthiest storm burst out full of dark and filthy human fluid (viva reader, post-scriptum survivor), and the city became unbecoming in which one-eyed pedestrians (cyclops and centaurs) turned against the other each claiming to know the absolute definition of the ideal lover, the original rules for original writing, or even as to what constitutes the body (and or the psyche) of the dead author and its dehydrated reader of an ideal swimming nation, or let alone their rare *chance encounter* (given that it ever occurs), rare as the rare chance encounter of the sewing machine and the umbrella on a Dadaist operating table, after which there was a long silence in the Carpathian Basin. Look, we must look at what we stare at, we must unveil the pool's curtain of lethargy and apathy and confront our pan-national, transglobal cyclops in shade, the dead novelist, pre mortem, explained, fixated at the tiny piece of pool, a blue aquarelle stretched out in front of him painted by his painter friend as a mini watercolour; you only have to gaze at something long enough to see that vividly, translucently, somewhat even artlessly, sin has already settled in there. Sin may be a heavy word in our summer discourse we try and weave here from lightness and light, perhaps it is a secret instead, a mystery, or simply, an accident, that which is there in front of our very eyes as nothing in disguise, until it gains the contours of the visible, the tangible, i.e. a living thing, as something, because everything that moves or lives with a long enough life span has an effect on everything that moves or lives if it moves or lives long enough to have an effect on things swimming within proximity, i.e. everything that lives long enough has the chance to fail, to lapse, to harm before it dies. At early dawn, the close of day when I morphed into you and you morphed into I, when the pool's fog enfolded the swimmers in a new, estranged euphoria, unfamiliar like the way loathing lovers enfold, antagonistically, in some uncanny heteroglossia (o loveless other, furious *furia*), as if we had been in the conversation before, *we* did as we were dictated and stared and gazed at the pool long enough and when we gazed long enough we noticed the first sign of flickering agitation of the water on the page, the agility of aqua, the apprehension on the sheet of the blue aquarelle. Look, anxious editor, it may sound trivial, the posthumous author adds, yet the fact that we have books, the fact that dead authors posthumously write and/or communicate, is beyond fantastical, one which the reader, or the swimmer, let alone the writer, for that reason, should not take for granted. In this implausible book, between pre and post writing, finally, until which point in time we are waiting, everyone will find their own swimming pool, their *fata sua*, but prior to that final finding (until then viva poor aporia) various versions of the same future will be written of the original, the infinite fate of *figura etimologica*, in other words a future with a fixed point of origin but an alternating, unsettling ending, fatal phantasmagoria. So let this book, bizarre and eccentric, be about the conceit of swimming pools, the infidelity of water, the betrayal of fluid homes. Krúdy, the fin-de-siècle swimmer, the horizontal author, in his *Dreambook* suggests that swimmers, via the daily practice of swimming, have the chance to reach what they have dreamt of, but what we dream of can give birth or shelter to the body of our darkest deepest dread, in other words to arrive home, given that *home* (or the *swimming pool*) is what we have dreamt (or been afraid) of, is not tautological, translucent or light. There is no fragmentation in water. Biography of water is fluid, never ending, it's *sans* conclusion, *sans* beginning, even *sans* soul or temperament or time. But what if the cartography of the swimming pool is drawn *sans* borders, *sans* measure, *sans* price. The topography of water, *sans* alpha or omega, *sans* chronology or frame. How do we read liquefied maps of lawlessness, of shame? The outline of floating islands, bodies of desire, the history of corruption, the swimmer's, the anti-lover's darkest, deepest crime? All optical phenomena are meant to be admired from a distance. O fata morgana. I have lots of recollections of swimming early winter mornings in the outside pool of the National Swimming Pool situated in the heart of the city on Margaret Island floating in fog. You had to swim out from indoor through a tiny water tunnel to arrive outdoor at the Olympic size pool always hazy, obscure, steamed up in the winter. The pool was named after Alfréd Hajós, the country's first gold medallist who won his first gold medal at the 1896 Games that were held in the Mediterranean Sea in which swimmers had to battle with the real elements and themselves, (the real elements i.e. themselves), who plainly pointed at the pool, when asked to reveal his secret. Dear curious columnist, cartographer of tour de force, of triumph. Where else could we learn to swim, while alive, other than in water. Later, by then an architect, when asked again to confess, he gestured again at the pool cloaked in fog and said his will to live, under duress, had overcome the ambition to succeed, to build, to overcome. And there is more to it. The pool has an old motel attached to it, in the old motel a secret room, Room 100, in which, according to the clandestine chronicle the nation clandestinely chronicles about, writer Krúdy in the early 1900s used to stay overnight in order to have a long snooze and sober up. From this room 100 that still exists, the posthumous Krúdy, who no more exists, sketched the first versions of his

*Dreambook* in which he depicts the pool milieu as the place of homecoming to an alternative home that also always superimposes peril, danger and hazard, a pool in which chlorine and thermal water can easily turn into human hair and blood. On the actual day, the posthumous author writes, the Island, in that time zone named Isle of Hare, a tiny landlet in the middle of the dark Danube, like the city's long chambered heart, flickered, effervesced like an oasis or mirage, hallucination of ideal fin-de-siècle fauna and flora, fake water, the secret isles of Ithaca or Eden. The speaking fountain was fountainously foaming, the national swimming pool colonised by pompous bathing and sunbathing pathos and bathos, the sun at its summit in the ideal blue sky when the animal, already half slaughtered, exsanguinated via its carotid artery and jugular vein, escaped the butcher's fatal strike causing havoc amongst the fragile, filmy figures of *femmes d'esprit* & *femmes savantes* (that of the undercover *angelus fatale*), who took the afternoon to walk around the Arboretum holding onto the elbows of their escorting conversationalists who were holding onto their walking sticks conversing about fate and time. And the bewildered pig, half pre-, half post mortem, ran around bleeding, squeaking, screaming amongst the yelling screaming crowd; the noise so deafening that the writer could not tell the scream of the butchered from the roar of the butcher. And when it was over there was no final word, the posthumous author warns, there was only silence. O swimmer, o bathos, wash your body for Thanatos, not Eros. The same routine, similar ritual: clip your toe nails, shave lower legs, wax bikini line. Love poems are diplomatic death poems in disguise. Death poems are love poems, unconcealed, veiled and amorously masked. But as fades the glowing orb of day, at early dawn, the close of day, when *I* begins to believe faithfully in *doubt* and the pastoral turns, first into denial, later into catastrophe, I saw what the fog was genuinely made of, the pool's fake tissue, skilful texture, in other words, what the fog *was* genuinely *not*.

And in this sinister hue, eerie illumination, for a fractured moment that did not last long but lasted long enough, we saw, as if apparition or as if in a scene of Greek bucolica, a group of swimmers gathering in water, their deltoid dark bodies coining a priceless configuration, as if by the swimmers' (well-practised) transubstantiation, figures in fog transfigured into pool's stunning symphony, while encircling, in a circle wholly part of this harmony, another phantom swimmer, her body, a spectre or a centaur, half-fog, half-aqua, out of air, out of despair, under and above the simulacrum pool simulating pool, caught in a tight ring of the swimmers' synchrony, and so one fluid moment to the next the mesmerising act, in front of our eyes, metamorphing from a co-shaped geometric butterfly into the blurred outlines of the ideal and impeccable crime. And a century later when the heavy curtain of fog lifted and the old continent felt all at once free, when we opened the newspapers and other unpublished local records of anonymous archives in which the vocabulary of the pool was new, altered and estranged, we saw that irregularities were regular, abnormalities normal, unfamiliarities familiar in the history of swimming; in wildlife lakes, in city parks, in lidos and local swimming pools. That day the sky was blue and the summer only just hatched, only just bloomed. Dear Simulator Swimmer, dear pool demon. Today swimming flew melancholically, the date: June, 1951. There was an early summer breath which made the outdoor sign, designed to invite, tremble in the wind. The blue tiled corridors freshly wiped were echoing with eerie gossip, muffled whispers, terrific chronicles. In the shower room I saw us clotheless, shameless, showering, cleansing our bronze bodies for life. But the pool, hiding in the public bathroom behind the pool, showered us with shame. And so, in our unsheltered shame we tried to hide with hands or towels what we had to hide. And the next day, or much later, the pool, *historia*'s, the heart's typewriter, commissioned by local, national and pan-national archives, continued its

fluid discourse, its own dictation so the next day or much later we were told to keep calm and then to shower and then to swim fast and even faster. And later, much later, because our will to live was greater than ambition, we began to forget. But as fades the glowing orb of day, at early dawn, the close of day, I, the idle swimmer, the phantom swimmer, the elastic swimmer without ending or beginning, noticed in the morning shower that my body had grown ancient, temporal, corporeal, final, in other words as old as the pool.
As old as alma mater.

[Pool letter 1.6 typed, Misc. vi]

Attention. Shower before entering pool.
Por favor ducharse antes de entrar a la piscina.

[*On the Poet's House*]

Paul calls it a *littlecry*. In Wonderland it's called
Pool of Tears. In our diluted poem, this water
narrative, it's named after Lacrima, the silent
swimmer's former fluid home. Either way, Paul
says, it's good to release the loathful, lustful lover
who holds so tightly onto the posthumous poet's
torso, photographing themselves with the dead
author in the phantom's final fluid homes, as if the
two, the animate and inanimate, were the ideal
couple, the co-joint twin, the lover and its ghost
(perhaps suggesting that the love they feel,
unfeeling, unthinking, apathetic, outlives time, or
perhaps as if they had always wished you to be
idle, timeless, immortal, while they were alive, a
sign of, the hopeless hopeful lover might
posthumously argue, pathological love, but
nonetheless *isn't it love* etcetera), as if this rather
cryptic encounter of the animate and inanimate
were the absolute chance encounter both reader
and writer had missed while they were alive. Here
the clever klaviatur would have typed the word
*embrace*, or even *fold*, for that reason but – not
even archaic Apollo's – torso can quite hold you in
their arms (because i. they are idle ii. they lack
divine limbs). They certainly can't enfold the fluid
swimmer, who, we posthumously think, was in
fact, while alive, a lucky fleer, the timely escapee
of such idolised embrace or fold, even though you
think their marble hearts (in absentia) ache only for
you. The posthumous poet, however, can't have a
littlecry either because they lack lacrimal glands.
So stick to friends, who can cry (given that they
don't cry with the cry of cyclops or crocodiles),
Paul also says, who speak with you, *vis-à-vis*, *tête-
à-tête*, eye to eye through their pool of tears, as if
the two of us, the two of you, set in an 2-shaped

sofa, were conversing, secreting tears, head to head, heart to heart, cor to cor (provided, that we, the conversationalists, possess a *cor*). My dear cordial converser. I noticed lately that one only has to mention swimming pools and around the round table friends open up their hearts, *vis-à-vis*, eye to eye, heart to heart, as if memory, like the tub or tap of collective history, were all at once unplugged, turned on, and countless accounts and recounts of swimming pools begin to spin around our round table of timelessness and time. Everyone has their version of *historia sua*, their unique stories of their own pool phantoms, pool appearances and disappearances, their own parables of pool phobia, tales of pool philia. The latest conversation, heart to heart, vis-à-vis, eye-to-eye occurred in the lift at work today when Fabienne who, slightly agitated and animated, (signs of which were enlarged pupils and lubricated eyes, symbols of involuntary internal emotions, such as sorrow, elation, love, awe or pleasure but similar symptoms can be caused by laughing or yawning), a nervous excitement triggered by the pool subject, recalled her own version of *La Piscine*, the movie in which Alain Delon features. The movie is set in the swimming pool in France in which the pool-scape conceals all the love and hate scenes, the place of betrayals, darkness and other unnameable contents, the kind of pool the swimmer, the lover is unfamiliarly familiar with or I should say the scene the swimmer always already knows. It is also where the drowning scene I watched much later in French with Portuguese subtitles, the only available version at the time, takes place in which the competitive, jealous lover, the young Alain Delon, *sans* soul, *sans* love, *sans* passion murders his rival by holding his body down (till the right time, till the end of his time, till eternity, till immortality, i.e. until the rigorous body reaches rigor mortis) in the dark of the pool. *Encerrado*, *são yo feliz agora*, the polyglot lover begged in the pool's familiarly unfamiliar language. *Vous ne voulez que tout. Et vous voulez tout maintenant. Me ajude. Me ajude.* Stop the foul game. Help me. Help me. Help me etcetera. When the murder is complete, in other words, post-climax, post-trauma, post-crisis, when the pre-mortem lover, in our case the poem, is by now posthumous, post-scriptum, post-joke, post-jest, that is, by which we mean horizontal, that is, finally at rest, a huge aeroplane cuts through the dawn sky right above the pool. In Fabienne's version the swimming pool, an alternative pool that rules with alternative rules, hermetic and sinister, is inhabited by the spirit of subtle paranoia, oppression and apprehension, and to prove her point she shows me her latest findings of laminated postcards by the young Slovakian artist Svarbová with stages of atmospheric shots of pastel-hued swimming pools with pristine walls and corridors covered with various prohibitions signs, from *attention, no diving* to *no drowning, no crying, no peeing in the pool*, a type of pool no character leaves that day. And so the plot finally just gets very dark. Although how much darker can darkness get, you may rightly wonder. Dear Paul, there is a liminal, other-worldly place in the North of England, a funny train station tavern called The Tap whose beer barrels sell to the weary traveller, the fluid flâneur, along with the usual variety of local ale and foreign lager, history and time; in the fin-de-siècle public chamber, the light, on a normal day, is sepia yellow, enveloping the crowd, muffling their private murmurs (from which tiny apocalypses have the chance to spring out and flee) about something almost audible. When they finish sharing anecdotes, exchanging histories, chronicles of shame, they'll sip up their last drop of Yorkshire ale and leave even more quietly through the back door. We call this secret back door the *last chance*

to exit the story, in other words to escape (it), in
other words, to survive (it). But dear Fabienne,
dear critic of fear. Panic makes irresolvable poles
of the globe, our domestic pool, reunite, and so our
own small scale fear, unquantifiable on the
international map of fears, too quantified. And so
in the film *La Piscine*, those characters who
survived the fatal scene, left (and so us too)
behind, stand at the edge of the pool, right above
the victim's tomb, seemingly, in death's
irrevocability, all reconciled. Now I'll never
know what you'd have been like; old, white-haired
and wrinkled, Penelope sighs. She gazes into the
darkness of the grave below for a second
and walks away into the sun.

[Pool letter 1.7 typed, Misc. vii]

no long breath holding no long breath holding no long breath

*Part Two*

On the Art of Tautologising

[Pool letter 1.8 typed, Misc. viii]

Attention. No means No.

[*Letter from Terry*]

And so to be able to perform nothing you need to provide the audience with a simple reading, Terry writes. Drama without drama, complication or crisis. It should be a no-performance, long enough (although how long is long enough you may rightly wonder, or more precisely how short is short enough to avoid lapsing, hurting, harming within the short time we have before we die) so people can come and go until they get bored or tired or simply aware of time. The weave of language and content has to be its own thing, no sense in decoration. The cut and paste of the unexpected echoes, the random, unfitting pieces will weave a fit architecture, a fabulous journey for the voice, our testimony of *no*. It is like my own deviant path to learning about the world – acknowledgedly partial and fragmented and infinite. And so, see, your empty swimming pool, your precious pool *sans* pool, *sans* water, like the no text, that which still remains a text with texture, made of living fabric, is textured of binaries, a kind of building that inherently carries, or I should say quietly confronts unbuilding within itself. This private inner conflict is what produces *nothing*, *our* inner no, because, needless to say, we must take care of it, in other words, we must feel *something*, in other words, one must care. No means no, that's right but our prohibitions, the bans and bars in and on our lives, chosen or given, do, with time, morph into affection. And so, vice versa, our deepest intimacy into obstinacy and so tight-lipped silence. But there is always hope for love. Hope is the last to go. I have no doubt. A yes to life is no to death. A yes to death is a no to life. A no to life is a yes to death. A yes to death is a no to life. A no to death is a no to life. A yes to death is a yes to life. The

syllogism is open, endless, infinite, if you like.
And so, since you have asked, we will perform
nothing as something in disguise masking it as
everything in disguise of nothing, made of and in
this world, a world that's partly and wholly part of
the other world, constituted from nothing, our non-
being, our no-thing, as partially and wholly part of
something, a paradox your own sadness is made
of, like the parable of the loathing lover, long
gone, still inhabiting you, or the permutation of the
phantom swimmer dormant, idle, still still in the
real swimmer, the carcass of the dead typist in the
(also already) dying author, the poet in absentia,
who does not exist, still set still in lotus pose at the
margin of the poem that exists, your most precious
thing, or like our own alter ego always already in
incognito, the way you too mute from the
mutability of you, or let alone the poem, the total
tautologiser, composed from the same and only
poem, that is, of nothing else other than itself, so
does nothing permeate from nothing, as your pool
from the many inner pools, permeates from
something, and being constituted of something, a
living thing, like the pool, or the poem, or the
paradox of sadness in you, it is made of our own
emptiness, it's made of us. So bon courage. And
she signs off with *love, Tiresias.*

*[On Another Death of the Moth]*

And so I watched the moth stuck inside the apocalyptic ceiling's circular lamp in the bathroom for a long time, although how long is long enough you may rightly wonder, or more precisely how short is short enough to avoid lapsing, hurting, harming within the short time we have before we die. The moth, the tautologised moth, tautologised because of the endlessly repeated version of its own death in the history of art, this moth, that one time was another moth yet the same moth who lives its life in the same *modus vivendi* as any other moths, which died many dystopian deaths, once, already posthumously, in Woolf's essay in 1942, an unusual modus mortis paradoxically caused by writing it all down, other times, already as post mortem, dehydrated parchment, flimsy post scriptum mourned by W. G. Sebald in the corner of a godforsaken East Anglian motel room, a small body of a life that went through a series of transubstantiations and permutations, the last time showing its fatal appearance in France during the Euro Final 2016, swarming with its many altered pre mortem selves into the entire football pitch, one of itself landing and ending its life on the bridge of Ronaldo's nose, the deadly moth, the live moth, the being non-being, is the mottephobic's worst nightmare one could say. It, the tautologised moth, while alive, was obviously drawn to the laser light with an inherent desire for or obsession about small, illuminated planets, and crawled in, secretly, one night, from the top, through the thin crack between the ceiling and the rim but in order to crawl out again it would have needed to take flight, for which there was very little room inside the lamp inside, that was outside, the space of the illuminated bathroom, inside the flat, inside the house, inside the street, inside the tiny Tunsgram life bulb. I tried to screw off this globe from the firmament several times to free the moth without success so instead I was involuntarily exposed to the slow death of the uninvited being, whose non-being I dreaded more than it being still alive. During its process of dying it went through various stages of metamorphosis in a hopeless attempt to survive, or I should say prolong its agony, inside the globe outside. At times it shrank its body closing its wings tight, as if to camouflage (with an inherent desire to be something or someone else), sometimes moved locations within the circumference, at other times it tried to fly or crawl in circles. And there were times when it thought it was no moth but glass. All repetitions, the cyclical life and death gestures were x-rayed, even enlarged, one could say like the small acoustic body of sound through water, maximised, through the orbicular glass. And with each day I was sinking further too in depression. It took a week for the moth to let go. The slowest week for both of us in which time slows down and fear speeds up. Because who could co-exist with an agonising being, the mottephobic's worst kind of horror, darkest dread, the liminal terror, or even hope, between being and non-being, knowing or unknowing what awaits every time you arrive or depart. And so one afternoon on my return to home inhabiting outside but situated inside, first thing was to check the state of the creature inside the lamp inside that was outside. It did not react to the source of illumination. The idle body of the moth, composed from the same and only moth, that is, of nothing else other than itself, its once rigorous, small, inaudible *yes* to life morphed into rigor mortis in which it decided to leave its dehydrated carcass for me in full glory, wings stretched open, antennae erect, the anatomy of the body, its whole structure inside, now stuck wholly inside for ever, visible. Trachea, aorta. And there, there, its long chambered heart, as if still, moving, a tiny bit, as if it were saying: Death no death. I am here. It's a jest.

[Pool letter 1.9 typed, Misc. ix]


Pool closed after dark pool closed after dark pool closed after

[*On the Glass Poem*]

But what in pool does the pure swimmer, the absolute swimmer, faithful with an absolute faith in herself, being, swimming in this fluid world, in pool's primal milieu which we enter, each time we enter, with the same pre-natal euphoria as if we were to begin all over again, as if the empty pool were our pre-semantic school where we learn our first alphabet from alpha to beta, in other words, from the beginning to the end, an elastic, fluid system of utterance, as if each letter or sound underwater were much more elongated, much slower, like elongated roars or cry of underwater swimmers in the history of photography or art, like vocal shadows and shades, in which our acoustic bodies were not quite yet lost, heard or found, and who at times of crisis returns to this private water lexis, to quiet conversations about the climate of the pool, namedropping names of pools inside and outside the pool, privileged to enter pool's ongoing underground discourse, like the good reader incognito, who at catastrophic times profits only from the same and only book during their short or long-lived life, although how long is long enough you may rightly wonder, or more precisely how short is short enough to avoid lapsing, causing harm within the short time we have before we die, returning to the pool *sans* pool, admire? Dear fearer of desire, by which we mean ambition, by which we mean a cosmological or *celestial* drive, bon courage. Márai, the invisible prophet, the hooded writer in exile inside and outside, spends most of his life inside the inner domes, outside history and yet wholly inside his own story, in the historic mist of Turkish steam rooms in Buda away from the public performing, as he writes, the absolute aquatic thinking. For the same reason, Ottlik, the aquatic author, who believes in a world unreal, imaginary, sets his novel in the fin-de-siècle Lukács

Spa thinking he too was a protagonist, intangible, unseen. Or take silent Socrates, for another example, who, set in lotus pose at the edge of the pool, decides to write his syllogisms, *sans* paper, *sans* concrete, on water. Dear mourner, dear (d)reader, what did Bloom, for that matter, waterlover, drawer of water, watercarrier, who had learnt to swim like a swimmer, write like a writer, arriving at the margin of the empty pool, the ruins of our civic space, our place of gathering for silent thinking, our long gone Agora, where time slows down and thought flows speedier in the fluid milieu of public banter about private catastrophes, our own imaginary final cataclysmic events whose outlines, we don't know why, but we don't yet know, mourn in this liquefied loss? Or think of Tiresias, as our anti paradigm, whose life begins or ends, ends or begins from a fatal gulp of water from a see-through glass; wasn't it already a warning, an incident we so often ignore moving linearly ahead or retrospectively reversing backwards in the history of coincidence? But dear idle admirer of chance, of accident. This otherworldly desire, passed on from swimmer to swimmer through the chronology of pools, may well have to do with the fluid body of water, the mutable psyche of aqua, the permeable materia prima, the contourlessness of the swimming body in water, the length and width of our own body in water, a desire, a longing, elastic, as long and as elastic and as wide as the pool, a self-definition, self-measurement, being defined and measured by the parameters of the pool, a longing to be pool. Or perhaps is it to do with, not water, but glass? They say it's an end of the swimming pool era. An era which will never return, for tautology, too, like the repetition of pointless aporia pleadingly addressing the loathing lover (even though it is hard to type such texts under duress), has exhausted its inner fountains and wells. Permutation of inner and outer pools, tiled inside, tiled outside, the incarnation of one's permeable inside, that can both live and die, die and live, live and live, die and die

at the same time, like the endless version of
the moth and its short or long lived life, immortalised,
immaterialised, or say our own intimate lives, like the
tautologised life of the Syrian swimmer, who,
escaping war, left her former body behind by
drowning in the Aegean Sea, but her new, estranged,
other self, unknown even to herself, miraculously reborn and so now qualified to swim (as if her eternal –
other – life was at stake) at the 2016 Rio Games, can
only practise such charms, such magic once in one's
linear lifetime. And so, the golden era is gone, no
doubt, and we are left with the poollessness of the
pool, our new and estranged pool with new laws, new
paradigms and pool parameters, a pool as yet
unknown, unfamiliar to us, unrecognisable, like the
once popular and populous corridors of Azure after
the Ukrainian nuclear disaster, a liminal site that exists
as a non/being, erased and yet memorised in our
collective minotaur's mind. And it's the end of an era
because, like the way liquid is *mortalised* by glass, our
poem too, our most precious thing, our glass house, in
which language, and our inner swimmer, are mortified
at being made see-through, translucent, at being
immortalised, by the prospect of gaining a living
shape, concrete contours, that is, that which will make
his or her body separate, stand out as part, lonelily
apart, with no promise of being wholly part. Art, the
posthumous Pilinszky, the stoic swimmer writes,
creates balance, movement from facts to reality
chronologically motioning from visibility to non-visibility, from a world that's lost or doomed,
unrealistic, absurd but still exists towards our inner
deity which, although it does not exist, is inherently
good, therefore *is* reality. And of course, mourning
what's gone is not good or real enough. So dear
mourner, dear dreaded reader, what did Bloom, for
that matter, waterlover, drawer of water, watercarrier,
arriving at the margin of the empty pool, the ruins of
our civic space, our place of gathering, our long gone
Agora, mourn in this liquefied loss? Do we mourn the

weather, the vineyards, and the warm tiles, tiled inside, tiled outside. The sluggish journeys, the sluggishness of the body itself, the slow-moving monstrum of the Southern Transdanubian train strolling by miniature stations across the continent to Trieste Bay where we watch, much later, on our nautical map, Aqua Pannonia sailing down the drain. Or perhaps the tangibility of all this. The intimacy of touching. Framing the world, outside, inviting it inside. As if it were the world outside, minimalised, a tiny Edmondson train ticket in Bloom's pocket, tucked inside, essential standard feature introduced in 1842 in England to make the world outside faster, more see-through, competitive and so to last longer, as if it were a mini cardboard internal pass to the other, outer world. And we miss, of course, time the wunderkammer, the pocket encyclopaedia maker, the catalogue of cosmic clutter. The museums of swimming pools, the dead metaphors, the archive of August mini meteors, the gallery of night crowds watching the sky above the pool, the fellow poet-torsos, the crowded catacombs, filthy mausoleums. The arboretums. And other oval, concave words like these. Their amphora bodies. Obsessive holder, collector of things. And of course we missed Noe. With her the slow, elongated moments of ark watching on the bank of the dark Danube or the river Thames, the kayaks' skilful carcasses, terrific pirouettes. Or maybe we missed sitting in lotus pose, *sans* desire, *sans* shadow, *sans* silhouette, at the margin of the poem watching agitation being born on the sheet as the century turned pathologically as the convex body turns too. And now, my hydrophilic friend, *sans* pool, *sans* water, should Bloom, left only with glass, entering the orangery of melancholy, in a puddle of nostalgia, simply forget? In the world's waiting room, hiding behind and within glass, wearing a new, unfitting swimming skin or self, should we join the forgetful crowd to become part, as apart but wholly part of the collective unhappiness, and if so is

the key in regathering in regret? A type of forgetting
into which like hypnotised centaurs, we submerge,
half-part of the underworld, half-apart, exercising a
difficult breathing exercise, some tragicomic version
of katabasis, longing for magna mater, for the cosmic
womb, the absolute hydrostatic equilibrium, for the
ultimate paradox, the one and only water discourse
which doesn't weigh, doesn't count and doesn't make
any sense or difference. O ever flowing Tap. O the
liminal glass on which *liquefied love* is cursorily
typed. O minuscule pools, half full, half emptiful,
duplicating the mourner into a bleak isle of mourners,
viva *moirai*, shrouded, dark gondolas. And in a half-
illuminated, sorrowful bacchanalia, the bizarre poem,
weaving its own final cataclysmic event, flows on,
half lament, half requiem:

[*On the Sepia Swimmer*]

And the next day, cutting through Watertown, the old
Buda district by tram *bathos*, our sepia swimmer,
bathed in self-pity and pathos, the nostalgia swimmer,
the homesick swimmer, nostalgic and homesick for
pool sepia, pool melancholia, feeling old and young,
visible and invisible at once, pre and past his or her
linear time, shrouded in a perpetual, diachronic gloom,
a municipal grief, mourning not so much civilisation
but some kind of synchronic, civic centre, the Zero
milestone – that used to be a gigantic concrete o in the
centre of town, they say, the focal point of fluid
thinking, what once was intimate or even domestic,
the place of belonging to some liquefied home, her
local pool, a kind of mourning like the way our no-
poem, the *nulla* poem, the (geometrically) pointless
poem mourns language, mourning perhaps the soft,
porous heart that used to exist inside her fellow
citizens, the random urban tête-à-tête, eye to eye, heart
to heart, the summer banters in which names of polis'
swimming pools are permanently familiar,
permanently and familiarly dropped, left behind and
picked up again like names of great-great-
grandparents or other safe paraphernalia of the
swimmer's psyche, a liquefied elegy or aquatic
lament, a grieving for fluid language games, for sunny
saturnalias, involuntary exchanges of equinoxing
words, among the fin-de-siècle corridors of Buda
pools, grieving the fin-de-siècle heart itself, the pool
within the eclipsed pool, the *mise-en-abyme* pool that
gives access to the sepia swimmer to swim through
chronology without time, or in fact, the pool itself, the
pool-in-itself, its *aw*ful, pointless presence, but most
of all grieving the regular correspondence with the
posthumous author, the hydrophilic friend, who sends
laminated postcards from the margin of the pool on a
life mission to approach its focal point, that is, from

the other end, the focal point of the poem's absolute
solitude, heart to heart, vis-à-vis, eye-to-eye. The last
unearthed cardboard card was meant to arrive from
Serbia on which Kosztolányi, the posthumous poet,
scribbled his notes down in the early 1900s. The
image on the back was *Sunken Europe*, and the
writing continues to be in note form about the author's
journey through small towns and villages in which
people would gather silently in small circles in an
inexplicably opaque mood. No feast, no loud dance,
no pig slaughter, there was silence, as if war,
Kosztolányi writes well ahead of his own life, had
occupied the air, because it's war that makes so little
noise or sound. Dear silent flâneur, there are moments,
while alive, when the global swimmer, the elastic
swimmer, like our hypothetical typist of language who
types his or her futuristic end in circles unable to think
of the right word, the right end, typing around the
globe, the meridian, our local bathos free of anguish
and pathos, who swims, also, as far as her own body
lasts, in circles, round around the meridian because
that is the only thing that makes sense of the
circularities of his or her own utterance, arriving at the
point of departure and starting from all over again,
swimming in the world in small cycles of swimming
pool lengths, expects something to happen, something
to bloom. To change. A moment of acceptance.
Coincidence or chance. Resisting resistance, in other
words. That things will stay as they are. Pool,
whirlpool of pools: chronology's laminated postcards:
today there is silence around the margins of the
swimming pool, its sepia presence gradually seeping
towards the edges of the Old Buda district. There are
no swimmers in or around the pool, perhaps because it
is Our Lady's day with all the city dwellers and
dryland flâneurs gathering elsewhere for the end of
summer's final festivities in town. But from the spot
in which we, posthumous swimmers (swim or) stand
or lie, from the aquatic flâneur's position, that is,
always already from the other end, Room 100, stood

out, partially a part, lonelily apart, with no promise of being wholly part, is visible, convex, comprehensible from either end; the view, from the outside and from the concave inside. And so we assume, the room is emptiful. And vice versa: from inside the room, half empty, half full, there is clear panorama on the dark Danube spiralling away into the distance both ways into a fluid *filatorium*. In this liquefied silkworm factory there sits Ghandi in a lotus pose spinning away Bombyx Mori in perfect meditation, oblivion, equilibrium, linearly, accurately, chronologically unremembering, un-apprehending, unravelling *ourstory*, from end to end *sans* complication, *sans* crisis, *sans* agitation. And so learn to be a water-angel, says the new ad for mineral water this summer painted on the side of the bus, the last sentence we think of before entering the laminated barber shop in which Attila the Buddhist barber, laminated too, has been already expecting us. Attila, who likes philosophising while trimming your hair, bantering away about our auto-nautical crises and other approaching cataclysmic events, for instance about drowning St Petersburg or erased Dresden, and or our historical entrapments, living in the wrong era or time zone and of the after-after-after-after-life, today says it's definitely the end of an era, no matter how much we insist it stays with us. The fall of swimming pools is a process irreversible. Because take, for our final example, the accident with the cataclysmic creature, a testimony to what he believes in, to the cosmic process of how something, anything, once part of the world, a-part, a lonely part, yet still a being part, can turn into non-being, de-part, with other words, into nothing, and still wholly part of something contributing munificently, organically, to our existing world. The pigeon, like your tautologised moth, Attila says, or the poem, or your pool, for that matter, your final resting place, your Ithaca misplaced on the nautical map, your most precious thing, lost in last night's summer storm, who thought it was invisible, left an imprint on his window glass that was visible, the imprint so perfectly legible that you could see the entire structure of its body in flight, in other words it became the *schema* of its own final movement. Attila (not the one who once already drowned in the sepia Tisza or his alter ego whose cervical spine was crushed by the slow train cargo on the Transdanubian line on December the 3rd, 1937), the Buddhist barber said that the holy spirit according to apocrypha was an eagle, by the way, and so if that's true our argument for signs of *deus ex machina* is a poor aporia. But who knows, who knows. And he showed me the photo of a replica on his mobile. Because if we were more hopeful, more optimistic, or even animated, we could think the specific pigeon, inanimate, was made of something divine, deific, or even celestial. This laminated pigeon, or the laminated poem for that reason, or I should say the combination of the two, your future printed pigeon poem, which soon will be thrown against the glass by the hypothetical wind, its anatomy, its own story x-rayed by the window, made a fatal navigational error thinking it was invisible, see-through, that it was glass. It didn't fully realise its body parameters, its own longing to be extended, or be something or somewhere else other than itself. Because, Attila also said, the aim is to discard *desire*. Look at the way I am trimming your hair, watch the motion of my hands. Don't break the fluidity of the movement. No time for marginalia, doodles of the heart, no time for lament, for accidents. Be persistent on the page and complete your time in a steady linear order in one single length.

[*On Matt's Spirit Duplicator*]

But now that our inner catastrophic lover is gone, and we are left with a dosimeter, a gas mask, a pair of aqualungs and the final task to compose our water poem *sans* water, to perform pool without pool, to chronicle disaster *sans* disaster, to write of catastrophe having missed our own, cataclysmic event, drifting without our doomed lover in pool's dystopia, writing writing from this other end, *sans* philia, *sans* heart, *sans* pool's safe paraphernalia, in a pool, our most precious thing, emptiful, typing the caricature of the poem, letter by letter on the intimate klaviatur, *sans* dread, *sans* desire or even phobia, a purposeless aperture *sans* catharsis, *sans* play, how will the empty swimming pool, our hollowed-out poem attract an audience. How will we fulfil our duty, the complex task with which we are left behind: to turn the concave poem into convex, how can we, from this ultimate no end, *viva life, viva death!* navigate, like the aquatic lettrist *sans* aqua, our lepidopterist *sans* love for moths or butterflies or our posthumous poet who cannot meet his own accident, the post-apocalyptic swimmer, pool survivor who missed his or her own *fata sua*, the lonely lover's body home through language through litter and letter as if your own short-lived life (although how long is long enough you may rightly wonder, or more precisely how short is short enough to avoid lapsing, hurting, harming within the short time we have before we die) were at stake. Dear typewriter, dear heart. Staring long enough at the tiny piece of blue aquarelle, Esterházy, the celestial swimmer writes pre mortem, but always already from the other end, swimmers, like the poem, or the script, who do not reach the margin in their own lifetime, i.e. the swimmer who *desires*, i.e. the poem, your most precious thing, a script with a centre, a text with *cor*, a porous heart, won't gain entry to the house of emptiness, left to repeat, length after length, line after line itself to and froing from end to end to find its final event, entrapped in its own desire to express, to say something, to endlessly address. So swim your heart *out*, while you can, as if your own, or the poem's, for that matter, final chance, its coincidence were at stake. In other words, your power is indeterminate. So betray what matters most, what's most intimate. Let the swimmer, the poem, the script terminate its own quiet cataclysmic event. Dear typewriter, dear heart, but if, by chance, charm or accident you reach a margin, moving from Alpha to our most private Omega, let the typing move backwards, and move gently from Omega to Alpha and when you have got to the *word ending*, type circularly, impulsively, accidentally, and start it all over again. Dear typewriter, *dear heart*. Type, if you must type, the feeling poem which when it feels it feels indifferent. Type, if you must, the absolute no poem, the global eco-poem of and about an eco-swimmer, the hollow swimmer, the recycler of nothing, the lover of lack, who swims in reverse on the page, our fluid aquarelle, carefully unthreading any thread in order not to leave a single symbol, mark, or trace behind, the miasmic swimmer who swims invisibly, in shade, and, like the poem, duplicate, permeates from nothing else other than itself. Write about an alternative lover who, without love, if you must love, learns to tautologise itself, to duplicate.

[**Pool letter 1.10 typed, Misc. x**]

To the pool →

## Acknowledgements

Earlier versions of these poems have appeared in various print and online publications:

A small fraction of the collection was published in *Poems from the Swimming Pool* (a chapbook by Constitutional Information, Sheffield, 2015).

'Pool Epitaphs' were published in *Pool Epitaphs and Other Love Letters* (Boiler House Press, 2017).

Earlier versions of various single poems appeared in: *English* (Oxford Journals), *Blackbox Manifold, Molly Bloom, Datableed, Para-text, Atlantis* (Spirit Duplicator, 2016), *The Wolf* and *Locomotive Journal*. An earlier draft of 'On Catastrophe' was part of a Camaradefest II performance and a collaboration with Astrid Alben performed in London, Camaradefest II, 2015; excerpts from 'On Catastrophe' first appeared in *The Wolf* Issue 35. 'On Matt's Spirit Duplicator' first appeared in *electric-wood-spectra*, the ecopoetry-pamphlet of ASLEUKI & Land2 Conference published by Electric Arc Furnace and enjoy your home press (2017). A previous versions of 'Hypnos and Hajnóczy' and 'The Mother' were published as part of a piece of 'Liquefied Polis' in collaboration with Elżbieta Wójcik-Leese in *Long Poem Magazine*, Issue 17, May, 2017.

An earlier version of 'Time How Short', expressly written for the sequence by Denise Riley, first appeared in *Pool Epitaphs and Other Love Letters* (Boiler House Press, 2017). 'For A, a sauterelle' was written by Adam Piette for my 40th birthday. Terry O'Connor's 'The second of September, a card from Switzerland' was performed along with 'Letter from Terry' as part of a collaboration-piece for The Enemies Project's *North by North West Poetry Tour* in February, 2017 in Bank Street Arts, Sheffield.

**Some notes on the poems:**

'Hypnos and Hajnóczy' includes references to J. W. Waterhouse's oil painting *Sleep and his Half-brother Death* (1874), Péter Hajnóczy's novel *Death Rode Out of Persia* (1979), W. G. Sebald's *The Rings of Saturn* (1995) and scenes from *Austerlitz* (2001), and Virginia Woolf's essay 'The Death of the Moth' (posthumously published in 1942).

'On the Swimming Pool' contains references to Roger Deakin's *Waterlog* (1999), T. S. Eliot's *Four Quartets*, William Empson's *Some Versions of Pastoral* (1935), Louise Johnson's article 'Almost a Revolution: The Cultural Centring of the Swimming Pool' (2004), and *Swimming Studies*, a swimmer's memoir by Leanne Shapton (2012). The poem also references snapshots from *Freedom's Fury* (2006) directed by Colin K. Gray and Megan Raney, a documentary on the 1956 Olympic semifinal water polo match between Hungary and Russia. Held in Australia, the match, which is known as the bloodiest game in Olympic history, occurred as Russian forces were in Budapest stamping out the 1956 revolution.

'Melancholy Swimmer' includes references, among many others, to Nietzsche's *The Birth of Tragedy* (1872) and *On Truth and Lies in a Nonmoral Sense* (1873), Edward Stachura's novel *Axing, or the Winter of the Forest Folk* (1971), the 2010 Norwegian film *King of Devil's Island* directed by Marius Holst, and Paul Celan's 'Meridian' speech (1960).

'Enunciation' includes references to Lisa Robertson's *Nilling* (2012), to Nicolaus Wynman's *Colymbetes, sive de arte natandi et festivus et iucundus lectu* (1538), a book on swimming, thought to be the first of its kind, to János Arany's ballad on *Ágnes* (1853), (in which the protagonist loses her mind, presumably from guilt, after murdering her husband with the help of her secret lover), and to the controversial figure of (Count) László Almásy (featured in *The English Patient*) and his mysterious (missing) document *The Unknown Sahara* (1935). The triptych-poem makes references to the Neolithic painting *The Cave of Swimmers* located in Wadi Sura in Gilf Kebir plateau of the Sahara, in southwest Egypt near the Libyan border which was discovered by Almásy in 1933.

'Rockenbauer, The Diver' explores snapshots of Pál Rockenbauer's documentary from the early 1980s entitled 'Buzos Hungaros en Aguas Cubanas' which he filmed in Hawaii with his Jacques Cousteau Divers' Group. There are also references to *Le Monde Du Silence* (1956), a documentary film co-directed by Jacques-Yves Cousteau and Louis Malle; one of the first films to use underwater cinematography to show the ocean depths in colour. The poem also includes references to Keats's 'On a Leander which Miss Reynolds, my Kind Friend, Gave Me' (1817), Cy Twombly's painting *Hero and Leander* (1985), Dezső Kosztolányi's *Sunken Europe (Elsüllyedt Európa)*, travelling documents he wrote between 1909-1935, and Christopher Marlowe's lines in *Doctor Faustus*, referring to Helen of Troy, or as Marlowe had it, 'Helen of Greece'.

'The *Mother*' points at various works, some of which are: *Apology of Socrates* by Plato; Géza Ottlik's novel *School at the Frontier* (1959); Sándor Márai's small collection of essays *Füveskönyv* (1943); André Kertész's photograph *Underwater Swimmer* (1917); David Hockney's *Swimmer Underwater* (1978), scenes and conversations from *A Bigger Splash*, a documentary by Jack Hazan featuring Hockney (1974); also lines from Elizabeth Barrett Browning's 'Aurora Leigh' (1856). There are also fragmentary references to Jane Howard's interview with Nabokov (*Life magazine*, 1964).

'Pool Epitaphs and Other Love Letters' points at three major artists' various artworks: Bosch's *The Garden of Earthly Delights* (1490-1510), Helen Chadwick's *The Oval Court* (1984-86) and Karine Laval's *Poolscapes* and *The Pool* (2009-2010); also her *State of Flux* (2013-2014), a series of short films the artist filmed underwater. The poem also makes references to Gregorio Allegri's *Miserere* (the setting of Psalm 51: 2) in Latin: 'Wash me thoroughly from mine iniquity, and cleanse me from my sin' (KJV); passages from Vasari's *Lives of the Most Excellent Painters, Sculptors, and Architects, from Cimabue to Our Times (Le Vite de' più eccellenti pittori, scultori, e architettori da Cimabue insino a' tempi nostri!*), a series of artist biographies (1550); Keats's *Lamia*, Part II lines 231-238; the declaration of faith in the 1672 Orthodox Synod of Jerusalem quoted by J.M. Neale in *History of Eastern Church* (Parker, Oxford and London, 1858); Walter Benjamin's essay 'Theses on the Philosophy of History' (1940, in: *Illuminations*, 1999); László Krasznahorkai's novel

*The Melancholy of Resistance* (1989) which was adapted into the 2000 film *Werckmeister Harmonies*, directed by Béla Tarr and Ágnes Hranitzky; essays on poetry and poetics by Ágnes Nemes Nagy, some of which in English can be found in *Ágnes Nemes Nagy on Poetry, a Hungarian Perspective*, ed. Győző Ferencz, (1998); and among many others, to Sebald, Celan and Attila József. There are references to Keats's *Letters* to John Reynolds (1818), Catullus' poem 'Odi et Amo' (*Carmina LXXXV*), and segments from Merleau-Ponty's essays in *The Visible and the Invisible* (1964).

'Fall of Pool' includes indirect references, among many others, to Roland Barthes' *A Lover's Discourse: Fragments* (1977); Derrida's *The Gift of Death* (1995) and *The Post Card* (1987) including references to snapshots from *Love in the Post*, a film interpretation of Derrida's book directed by Joanna Callaghan (2014); Aristotle's *Poetics*; Denise Riley's *Say Something Back* (2016) and *Time Lived, Without Its Flow* (2012). There are also direct references to Péter Esterházy's novel, *Harmonia Caelestis* (2000) and his 'pancreatic diaries' (2016) (post-modern snapshots on his illness, published a few months before his death) and 'the sinner', a collaboration with artist Miklós Szüts (2015); Gyula Krúdy's *Álmoskönyv* (1925); Dezső Kosztolányi's *Sunken Europe* (*Elsüllyedt Európa*), travelling documents he wrote between 1909-1935; Henri Bremond's *La Poésie pure* (1925-1926); James Joyce's *Ulysses*; and Judith Tucker's art series, *Tense* (2008); images partly reflecting on Friedrichroda pool, a pool where the artist's mother learned to swim and, coincidentally, where the 1936 German Olympic Team practised in the late 1930s. Other minor references in the sequence are: *La Piscine*, a 1969 Italian-French film directed by Jacques Deray, starring Alain Delon, Romy Schneider, Maurice Ronet and Jane Birkin; Lewis Carroll's *Alice's Adventures in Wonderland*; Mária Svarbová's new photo-series *In the Swimming Pool* (2016); interviews with poet János Pilinszky from 1979 reflecting on Rilke's renowned line that says: 'it's terrible that because of facts we can never get close to reality'; Matthew Cheeseman's 'Spirit Duplicator', the copier Matt owns and keeps in his office in Sheffield that used to print a purple, cucumber-smelling ink that supposedly caused intoxication when inhaled (*Spirit Duplicator*, a small press, was founded in 2015 by Matt, too); *Jesus Green Pool* (2005), a documentary made by Chris Cox and Steve Riches following the life cycle of an eighty-two year old open air swimming pool in Cambridge, and to various photographs on the 'Azure Pool' in Pripyat, Ukraine, closed soon after the Chernobyl disaster. In the rest of the sequence there are continuous references to previously mentioned work by Woolf, Walter Benjamin, Sebald, Celan, Márai, Ottlik, Krúdy, Merleau-Ponty and others.

**Debts and Dedications**

I would like to say a heartfelt thank you to Denise Riley and Adam Piette for the careful reading of the manuscript and for the continuous and tireless co-thinking and correspondences about swimming pools for the past few years. A thank you is also owed to Denise Riley for her epigraph 'Time How Short' expressly written for the pool poems which appears in this collection's second sequence. I am very touched by Adam Piette's 'sauterelle' which he wrote on the occasion of my dreaded 40th birthday which fell on a leap year in 2016 so it was a double celebration and misery…from whichever point you are looking at it. A debt is also owed to Adam for enduring the idea of appearing as various Adams in the book; most scenes based on half-truths as that is the nature of poems. Another thank you goes to my friend Terry O'Connor for the piece 'The second of September, a card from Switzerland' which she offered to write for the third sequence as well as for our conversations on theatre and performance which I have incorporated into poems in 'On the Art of Tautologising'.

I am very grateful for Karine Laval, whose generous offer of her artwork *Untitled #7, 2002* (from *The Pool* series) has allowed its being incorporated into the cover of this book.

Many thanks to Tony Frazer and Shearsman Books for publishing the work. It's been a great pleasure to work with Tony again.

Special words of thanks are owed to Miklós Ferencz for his sensitive and mega-sophisticated work on the cover design and interior of this rather labyrinthine book as well as to John Hall and Allen Fisher for their critical comments; and for John's generously productive reflections on the poems in the making.

I would like to say thank you to my mother, the former gymnast, whose 'adventures' in Hévíz Spa I recycled in 'On Fear' and whose sheepdog, Panni features in 'The *Mothe*r', too; to my sister Hajni, for all our (swimming) times together; and to Szabi, Péter, András and (little) Ági; Csaba the perpetual aquatic flâneur; Noémi and for our boat trip to Badacsony which inspired parts of 'On the Glass Poem'; Madeleine (who apparently *almost* became a swimmer) and for our Danube trip; Paul, who truly ran into the Danube one hot summer 'semi-clothed' in Budapest; Alice and for her ruined swimming pools in *Midland* (2014) and Vicky for her kindness; Sokratis (who sometimes morphs into Socrates in the pool poems) and for our Athens adventures; Ethel for her stoic wisdoms; Fabienne for *La Piscine*; Isabel for our swims in the North Sea and Tess for our sea times together at Wells and Berwick; Vera, my Budapest friend, the Balaton enthusiast and Geraldine and Alan and for their Guardian Bay scenario. I am grateful to Emese (who features in 'Rockenbauer'), my university friend from Budapest, a former professional swimmer, who taught me how to swim 'properly'; she still owes me a lesson on the flip turn. Nonetheless, I am dedicating this book to all swimming pool lovers: to former swimmer and Oxford rower Louise whose Catalan article I refer to in 'On the Swimming Pool'; Ellen for Keats; Anna, who really saved the life of the young calf in 'Melancholy Swimmer' and in real life; Kate for poetry and friendship; Attila, my former hairdresser in Budapest whose pigeon incident I have recycled in 'On the Sepia Swimmer'; Dorothy who is happier to compose 'in' and 'on' water. This book is also for other pool lovers such as Judy and Harriet, Sue, Kaarina, Katherine & JT and also for Sasha because this book is about swimming pools and friendship, too, and if that stands this book is for Phil who 'in theory' loves swimming, too. Another thank you goes to all those friends who added to the content of this book with their own swimming pool narratives whose names I have not mentioned here: the list is simply endless. But this book also warmly addresses those whose swimming pools, for various reasons, could not be included in the collection. And so the pool poems in here sincerely reach out to Anna Jerram. And naturally these poems are offered to Alex, Ben, Vera, Joe, Bryn, Karl, Loma, Sam, Peter, Jenny, Tim, Amy, Lorenza, Lewis and Becky (and *so* many others) for the endless laughter, support and fun.

And I am hugely thankful for swimming pools in general, for their existence, the solid/fluid space they offer to the swimmer: specifically for Császár Komjádi Swimming Pool in Budapest with Krúdy's Room 100 still existing, for Mányoki Pool, my local pool in the XI district in Buda, for Goodwin Pool and Ponds Forge in Sheffield, for Jesus Green Pool in Cambridge, Norwich's University Pool at UEA, Lukács Spa in the XII district situated right next to Komjádi Pool, which has been a cultural, literary and philosophical hub for more than a century for artists and writers, Budapest National Alfréd Hajós Pool on Margit Island, and for the existence of my childhood summer pool, Lake Balaton, where I learnt to swim with my sister Hajni and where we swam every summer. We still do.

These water poems are dedicated to the memory of my father, the former kayaker and Danube lover.

Ágnes Lehóczky is a poet, scholar and translator originally from Budapest. Her poetry collections published in the UK are *Budapest to Babel* (Egg Box Publishing, 2008), *Rememberer* (Egg Box Publishing, 2012) and *Carillonneur* (Shearsman Books, 2014). She was the winner of the Arthur Welton Poetry Award 2010 and the inaugural winner of the Jane Martin Prize for Poetry at Girton College, Cambridge, in 2011. She was Hungary's representative poet for Poetry Parnassus at Southbank Centre during London's Cultural Olympiad in 2012. Her collection of essays, *Poetry, the Geometry of the Living Substance*, was published in 2011, and her libretto commissioned by Writers' Centre Norwich & The Voice Project was performed at Norfolk and Norwich Festival 2011. She co-edited *Sheffield Anthology; Poems from the City Imagined* (Smith / Doorstop, 2012) with Adam Piette. Her recent pamphlet *Pool Epitaphs and Other Love Letters* was published by Boiler House Press in 2017. She is currently co-editing *Wretched Strangers*, an anthology of poets' writing on transnationalism, out from Boiler House Press in Autumn, 2018. She is Lecturer in Creative Writing at the University of Sheffield.

www.ingramcontent.com/pod-product-compliance
Lightning Source LLC
Chambersburg PA
CBHW040301170426
43193CB00021B/2976